Order and Chaos

Order and
Chaos

laws of
energy and entropy

stanley w. angrist
loren g. hepler

drawings by ed fisher jr.

BASIC BOOKS, INC., *publishers*

new york / london

© 1967 by Basic Books, Inc.
Library of Congress Catalog Card Number: 67–17388
Manufactured in the United States of America
Designed by Ed Fisher, Jr.

preface

"It looks full of hard words and signs and numbers, not very entertaining or understandable looking, and I wonder whether it will make people wiser or better." So wrote a cousin of Josiah Willard Gibbs when she happened onto a copy of his most famous paper on thermodynamics lying on his desk. In this book we have taken great pains to eliminate as many of the "hard words and signs and numbers" as possible and still capture the essence of thermodynamics. We have tried to make the subject both understandable and entertaining, while pointing out some of the ways in which it has made life better for man. We believe that the story of the development and applications of thermodynamics is as interesting as it is important, and for that reason we have written this book. To paraphrase an old saw, "Thermodynamics is too important to be left to the thermodynamicists."

Along with telling about the laws of energy and their applications, we have told about the lives of some of the men who have contributed most importantly to our subject. In addition to the technical applications that are generally associated with thermodynamics, we have written about cultural implications in such diverse fields as poetry and the origins of life. Our treatment of all of these subjects has been influenced by Robert Louis Stevenson's dictum that "There is nothing like a little judicious levity."

It is a pleasure to acknowledge the many people who have assisted us in writing this book. First, we thank the readers of our early drafts who told us candidly what they thought was good and bad: Professors Richard Schoenwald (history), Ralph Drury (architecture), and Shirley Angrist (sociology) of Carnegie Institute of Technology, Dr. Jozsef Lukacs of the Semiconductor Research Laboratory in Budapest, and Lieutenant Colonel George T. Hankins, USAF Retired. In addition to chapter-by-chapter comments, Colonel Hankins also provided us helpful hints on the art of writing humor.

Much of the total impact of this book is due to Professor Ed Fisher, Jr., who both designed and illustrated it in a way that we feel is in perfect tune with the text. Miss E. Jean Stiles and Mrs. Dorothy Ponsetto typed the manuscript in a most careful manner.

Finally, we acknowledge our wives and children who have contributed in the most important ways of forgiving our absences and excusing our far-away thoughts.

S.W.A.
L.G.H.

Pittsburgh, Pa.
March 1967

contents

Order and

Chaos

chapter one
the
energetic
energeticists

The concept of culture is frequently used to distinguish men from animals. One way to interpret this concept is to view man as having extensive control of his environment. He has the ability to influence and guide nature to satisfy his needs and desires. This ability is not unlimited, but the progress of culture is characterized by the increase of man's ability to control the world in which he lives.

We may distinguish, as many anthropologists do, the first stage of cultural development as the era in which the human organism itself was the principal source of energy in the culture system; in this era wind, water, and fire were insignificant energy sources. This stage can be considered to have begun with the origin of man himself and to have ended with the first cultivation of plants. Leslie A. White, an anthropologist, assumes that culture (in this sense) began about one million years ago and he dates the beginning of agriculture at about 10,000 years ago. Thus the human-energy stage of cultural development in which human energy was the only energy source comprises about 99 per cent of culture history so far. He also notes that during this first culture period man subsisted almost wholly upon wild food—differing very little in this respect from the lower animals.

As long as man could not, and for ages on end did not, develop beyond his personal capacity for doing work of about 1/30 horsepower, culture systems were severely limited in the level which they could attain. Eventually man found a way to augment his energy resources, thus being able to raise his cultural level above what we may call "the one manpower level." The breakthrough

was achieved when he was able to cultivate plants and domesti-
cate animals. That is, he was able to harness solar energy in
nonhuman biological forms, such as plants and animals.

It is necessary to recognize the profound difference between
man's early utilization of wild plants and animals and his later
domestication of animals and raising crops. When man began
systematically to raise animals and plants, he effectively began to
harness and control solar energy to produce food, clothing, and
mechanical power. In short, he increased the production of needed
goods and services per unit of human labor. Furthermore, these
sources of energy were on a more predictable basis than when he
simply depended on the gathering of wild plants and the hunting
of wild animals. Thus culture advanced as a consequence of the
increase in the amount and dependability of energy harnessed
per year.

Playing a key role in the raising of man's culture and closely
allied with his control of energy was the development of tools.
Man's domestication of animals and his progress in agriculture
were only possible because he learned to develop certain tools.
Use of a stick to dig edible roots, an ox to draw a plow, or a simple
mill to grind corn are examples of some of the tasks man was able
to carry out with his first tools.

Wilhelm Ostwald, a German chemist, has pointed out that the
tool is related to the control of energy because primitive man had
only the chemical energy of the food stored in his muscles. When
man took a club in his hand, he increased the radius of his arm so
that he could apply his muscular energy more usefully. Ostwald
also pointed out that the crossbow permitted man to store energy
for long periods of time—thus adding another dimension to his
control of energy.

Since man originally had only his own muscular energy available to him, it was most important when he learned to concentrate
that energy effectively. Edges and points delivered energy to
small surface areas so that materials that would not yield to the

fist or the club parted readily when attacked with the sharp-edged stone or the piece of flint set in a crude wooden handle.

Man realized that for accomplishing certain tasks some of his tools could be combined to produce a device many times more effective than either of the tools which went into the combination. The sword or spear, for example, combined the increased length of the club with the ability to concentrate energy of the edge or the point. The development of these combination tools was the beginning of the end of the human energy stage of the development of culture.

Nature has presented man a world full of energy; a tiny but growing fraction of this energy is being brought under his control. To control energy effectively so that it may serve his needs, man must understand the rules that govern the utilization and transformation of energy.

In this book we mostly tell about how in the last 200 years man has reduced his observations and experiences to scientific laws—the laws of thermodynamics—and how he has applied these laws to the world around him. The fundamental concepts of thermodynamics are deceptively simple; yet they provide the foundation for one of the most general physical theories of modern science.

Three unifying ideas form the core of thermodynamic theory and in the chapters that follow we shall explore how these ideas arose historically and what they imply for us today. These precepts are:

1. *Energy*. All matter has energy and energy is never created nor destroyed.
2. *Equilibrium*. Events tend to move predictably toward a state of equilibrium.
3. *State*. Matter in equilibrium can be described by specifying a limited number of observable characteristics.

Thermodynamics is called a *macroscopic* science because it is not concerned with the individual molecules, atoms, or electrons that make up matter. Its truth, therefore, does not rest on present or future theories that describe the *microscopic* state of matter. The quantities utilized by thermodynamicists can either be measured or calculated from observations made in the laboratory on pieces of matter of reasonable size.

In attempting to tell this story we have elected to stress concepts rather than equations, principles rather than specifics. There are already excellent books on the details of thermodynamics. Our goal is not to make you, our readers, into thermodynamicists; we would, however, like to give you a feeling for the intent and the universality of the laws of thermodynamics.

Scientists are frequently portrayed as rigid, unemotional creatures who put aside all passions and let reason and logic govern all their actions. Whether for good or ill, this is untrue. One of the fascinations of science is *telling* what you have found, not just *finding* it. Thus when a new idea appears that might make it necessary for some scientists to retract or change their previously stated public views, it is only natural that the new idea may be received with something less than unbounded enthusiasm. It is precisely this kind of situation that has caused some scientists to give shameful exhibitions of bad manners, which frequently include scurrilous personal attacks.

In this chapter we introduce *some* of the cast of characters who have contributed to the development of thermodynamics and its present applications. A few of these men have engaged in public scientific wrangles as described above; some have had interesting lives for other reasons. Some important thermodynamicists are not mentioned in this chapter or even later in the book; we have been selective rather than comprehensive.

Antoine Laurent Lavoisier (1743–1794) succeeded spectacularly in nearly everything he undertook. He is generally recognized as the founder of modern chemistry, the demolisher of the phlogiston theory of combustion, an early worker in the fields of metabolism and nutrition, an expert in the compounding of gunpowder, and, alas, a conscientious and honest citizen who wanted to improve his country. His scientific accomplishments brought him and his laboratory to the attention of savants throughout the world. His desire to make his country a better place caused him to lose his head to the French Revolution at the age of fifty-one.

In 1775 Lavoisier was appointed to the Gunpowder Commission of France in order to try to eliminate the unchecked corruption that had taken over the existing supply system. After he was appointed to the Commission, Lavoisier moved into the Paris Arsenal where he established a private laboratory with his young attractive wife as his assistant. At his own expense he fitted workrooms with scientific apparatus and opened their doors to any scientist who wished to communicate with him and learn of his experiments. As his fame increased, his laboratory became the meeting place for many of the renowned of the scientific world: Priestley from England, Franklin from America, Ingenhousz from Austria, and Fontana from Italy.

Lavoisier encouraged other young men to visit his laboratory to witness demonstrations and occasionally to assist him. One of the young men he hired to work for him was Éleuthère Irénée Du Pont. During the Revolution Éleuthère escaped from Paris to the United States. Utilizing the advanced knowledge of gunpowder gained in Lavoisier's laboratory, he set himself up in the powder business in 1802 on a small tract of land near Wilmington, Delaware.[1]

Lavoisier's desire to help his country had manifested itself even before he became a gunpowder commissioner. In 1768 he bought a share in the *Ferme Générale* or "Tax Farm," which raised taxes rather than crops. The chief causes of the Revolution that took Lavoisier's life were the unremedied social evils of the eighteenth century. For hundreds of years France had an unsound fiscal

---

[1] *It is rumored that remnants of this original business remain.*

foundation. Her rulers did not know how to levy just taxes and her people payed the unjust ones with great reluctance.

Since the fourteenth century an exemption from taxation had been granted to the nobles and the holders of certain offices that could be purchased. The government "farmed out" the collection of taxes to the *Ferme Générale,* who were mostly hated as robbers by the tax-paying people. The members of the Tax Farm also formed a company of financiers who bought from the government the privilege of collecting certain indirect national taxes and customs duties. The government required that the Tax Farm deliver in advance so much revenue each year. The taxes might yield more or less than this amount. The more they collected, the more the Farmers stood to gain.

As a member of the Farm, Lavoisier instituted numerous reforms and efficiencies. One of his reforms, as administrator of the district of Clermontois, was to relieve the Jews of a tax called *pied fourchu* or cloven hoof. This tax was continued elsewhere for a considerable period of time.

The Tax Farm lease drawn up in 1786 did not run for its full term because of the outbreak of the Revolution, since the Farm was suppressed by the National Assembly in 1791. Its liquidation was entrusted to six of the Farmers. Lavoisier was not one of the six and his association with the Farm terminated.

In 1794 Lavoisier was arrested for his earlier membership in the Tax Farm. He was accused of adulterating tobacco with water by Jean Paul Marat, a frustrated scientist and one of the leaders of the Revolution. The Tax Farm had controlled tobacco processing as well as tobacco taxes. Actually, Lavoisier had introduced the practice of moistening the leaf to a standard moisture content to make it less brittle. Since tobacco was sold on the basis of dry weight, there seems to have been no intent to defraud.

Legend has it that at Lavoisier's trial Judge Coffinhal remarked, "The Republic has no need for scientists. Let justice take its course." Ihde notes in *The Development of Modern Chemistry* that this statement expressed something of the prevailing attitude, but the words were never actually spoken. We also note that while the harsh attitude of the Revolution toward science was certainly important to Lavoisier, on the whole science benefited from the Revolution. Just as in embarrassingly recent times, much of the benefit was derived from the recognition that science contributed to military power rather than from a love of knowledge. Some of the people who engaged in the early bloody excesses of the Revolution established the École Polytechnique; among this noted school's staff and students were Laplace, Lagrange, Berthollet, Fourier, Gay-Lussac, Carnot, Lamé, Thénard, Dulong, and Petit.

On May 8, 1794, Lavoisier was guillotined and his body thrown into a nameless grave in Parc Monceaux. Lagrange is said to have remarked the next day: "Only a moment to cut off that head and a hundred years may not give us another like it." Many historians blame Lavoisier's death on the nearly complete silence of the other members of the Academy of Science prior to his execution. Certainly more could have been done. Two years after his death the French government reversed the decision of the Revolutionary Tribunal and an impressive funeral ceremony with much oratory was held to commemorate his passing.

It is well established that people with widely differing backgrounds and positions have made significant contributions to the theory of heat and energy. Consider the following list of contributors to the science and practice of heat: (1) a spy for the British government in the employ of General Gage, who was British Commandant in Boston at the time of the American Revolution, (2) the Secretary of the Province of Georgia in the British Foreign Office in 1779, (3) the Undersecretary of State for the Northern Department in the British Foreign Office in 1780, (4) a lieutenant colonel in the King's American Dragoons, (5) a Knight in the court of George III, (6) a British spy in the court of the

Elector of Bavaria, (7) the founder of the Munich Military Work-house, (8) the designer of Munich's English Gardens, (9) a lieutenant general in the service of the Elector of Bavaria, (10) a member of the Polish Order of St. Stanislaus with the rank of White Eagle, (11) a Count of the Holy Roman Empire, (12) the founder of the Royal Institution, (13) a foreign associate of the French Academy of Sciences, and (14) Lavoisier's widow's second husband. Although this list reflects an extremely wide range of interests and occupations, it is nonetheless a list of accomplishments and positions held by one man! His name was Benjamin Thompson, an American born in 1753 to a simple farm family in Woburn, Massachusetts.

His life, as one can imagine from the preceding list, was a fascinating series of adventures of a brilliantly creative, hard-working scientist-politician. As we shall observe, he was also a consummate opportunist who had little regard for the sensibilities of others. Space will permit us to touch on only a few of his activities.

Thompson had made up his mind early not to remain a simple farm lad. At the age of nineteen he married a wealthy widow eleven years his senior. Shortly after his marriage he began to collect information for General Gage, then the British Commandant in Boston. He also helped to return deserters from the British garrisons. These activities did not endear him to his neighbors, who were beginning to tire of George III's rule. With the local Committee of Safety hot on his trail, he had to flee—leaving his comfortable thousand-acre estate, his wife of two years, and their baby, Sarah. He never went back.

In March, 1776, the British position in Boston became untenable. Thompson, who had continued his spying for General Gage, fled to Nova Scotia and then London. He received a commission from George III to raise a regiment of the King's American Dragoons. By the time his regiment was complete, the war was nearly over and his combat duty consisted of razing a village church on Long Island so that he might use its timbers for fortifications.

In September, 1783, the war ended and London was soon clogged with people who had picked the wrong side. Thompson got his Dragoons transferred from an American regiment to a regular British regiment. His lack of combat duty did not stop him from asking George III to promote him to full colonel and after some hesitation the King complied. Colonel Thompson then left for the Continent.

While touring Europe, Thompson secured a letter of introduction to the Elector Karl Theodor, reigning monarch of Bavaria. Upon presenting his credentials to the Elector, he was warmly received and almost immediately appointed to be aide-de-camp to the Elector. This was but the beginning of the honors he was to receive in Munich.

The first task Thompson undertook in his new position was the complete reorganization of the poorly trained and badly administered army. This task he did with fantastic efficiency and thoroughness; he even studied the thermal conductivity of cloth so that he might select the material that would make the most suitable uniforms. This was part of his plan to keep the soldiers warm and happy for the least cost. He did the same type of analysis on the food the army consumed and developed menus to provide the most nutritious meals at the lowest expense. Thompson was highly motivated in these endeavors, since the Elector permitted him to keep whatever funds he saved in running the army.

As soon as Thompson had improved the army, he turned his attention to the beggars of Munich. Having determined the best kind of cloth for army uniforms, he found that he could not buy this cloth from the army's usual suppliers. He therefore started what he called a military workhouse. On New Year's Day, 1790, Thompson used the reorganized and now well-disciplined army to arrest every beggar in the streets of Munich.[2] These people were then employed in the workhouse to manufacture cloth for the army. There they were given warm rooms and hot and nourishing meals. The workhouse soon prospered, and in addition to keeping the beggars off the street and the army warm, it turned a handsome profit for the Elector (and presumably Thompson).

The next year the Elector named Thompson a Count of the Holy Roman Empire, whereupon Thompson took the name Rumford— using the former name of the New England village in which he first experienced success.

Rumford, as we shall now call him, also operated a hospital for the poor and another institution in a quite handsome building about which he maintained a discreet silence. According to Gouverneur Morris, the American Ambassador to France, this house was "built by the State for ladies to live in privately and is the most superb building in Munich. . . . In England this would be called a strong legislative declaration of unchasteness." Without doubt, Count Rumford thought of everything.

While in Munich, Rumford started his experiments on the nature of heat, foodstuffs, light, chimney fireplaces, and other household items. His famous cannon-boring experiments, about which we say more later, were carried out in the Munich Arsenal. The military workhouse included a kitchen designed by the Count with a stove that was certainly the precursor in many respects of the modern kitchen range. His attention to detail is carried to a point where it approaches the ludicrous in some of his writings. On eating pudding:

[2] *The third English edition (1797) of Thompson's essays is in old script with the long* f*-like* s. *This typography sometimes adds interest to an otherwise dull passage. Commenting on the excellent health of the Munich beggars he wrote: "They were for the moft part, ftout, ftrong, fturdy, beggars, loft to every fenfe of fhame."*

The pudding is then eaten with a spoon each spoonful of it being dipt into the sauce before it is carried to the mouth; care being had in taking it up, to begin on the outside, or near the brim of the plate, and to approach the center by regular advances, in order not to demolish too soon the excavation which forms the reservoir for the sauce.

Sometimes the Count thought he had not made himself understood and he hastened to eliminate any uncertainty: "And first of all, the throat of the Chimney should be in its proper place; that is to say in that place in which it ought to be."

The Count was something of a double-standard man in his personal life. He forbade his daughter from marrying on at least two occasions, although in one instance her suitor was also a count of some standing. He was not, however, ashamed to acknowledge his paternity of a child born to a countess in Munich.

Having straightened Munich out about as much as he cared to, Rumford left Munich for London in 1798. His departure for London was not viewed as an unmitigated disaster by a great many people who had come to detest him. They held this attitude partly because they were jealous of the Count's accomplishments, but mostly for the arrogance with which he acted. He had been appointed Ambassador to London from Bavaria, but was not acceptable to the Crown as he was still a British citizen (and they were not quite sure for whom he was spying). So, without much else to do, he founded the Royal Institution and hired a country boy of twenty-two by the name of Humphry Davy to work in the laboratory. Davy's later scientific successes made the Royal Institution a power in Great Britain.

Once Rumford assured himself that the Royal Institution could get along without him, he left London to tour the Continent. In Paris in 1801 he met and courted Madame Lavoisier. His courtship was hindered because Napoleon was taking no chances with this British citizen, scientist or not. In 1805 Madame Lavoisier and Count Rumford were finally married in a wedding hailed far and wide for the unusual qualities and reputations of the principals. A London newspaper caustically reported the event as follows: "Married: In Paris, Count Rumford to the widow of Lavoisier; by which nuptial experiment he obtains a fortune of 8000 pounds per annum—the most effective of all the Rumfordizing projects for keeping a home warm."

The Comforts of a Rumford Stove

Figure 1–1
James Gillray honored Count Rumford in at least two of his Rabelaisian drawings. This sketch, published in 1800, shows the Count in an exposed position enjoying the pleasures of a Rumford stove.

The match was not a lasting one. Madame liked to entertain with parties and soirees; the Count longed for quiet hours of contemplation to write and experiment. Their fights became more spectacular, until finally in 1808 he moved to new quarters. He continued his researches there and in 1811 sent for his daughter, Sarah, after a separation of twelve years. Shortly after she arrived she was sent off to Switzerland to spare her the humiliation of sharing the feminine honors of her father's household with someone who was alluded to as the "flower lady." This woman, who was not a servant, took charge of the flowers, illumination of the house, and other needs of the Count.

Count Rumford died in 1814. He left his plain gold watch to Humphry Davy, all his books, plans, and designs relating to military affairs to the government of the United States (something of a surprise), and a thousand dollars to Harvard University to endow a chair in physics. His grave is tended by Harvard University, which is not bad for a man who once wrote a paper entitled: "Of the Excellent Qualities of Coffee and the Art of Making It in the Highest Perfection."

The four-year-old boy shook his fist at the man splashing water on the ladies rowing on the lake, shouting: "You beastly First Consul, stop teasing those ladies!" The First Consul the boy shouted at was Napoleon; the boy, Nicolas Léonard Sadi Carnot, was the eldest son of Lazare Carnot, Napoleon's Minister of War. Fortunately for the development of thermodynamics, Napoleon roared with laughter.

Until he was about sixteen, Sadi's education was directed by his father, who in addition to being an excellent military organizer was a first-rate mathematician. Sadi entered the École Polytechnique in 1812—the year that Napoleon's fortune took a downturn. After finishing his studies there in 1814 he entered the army engineers. Sadi had no taste for the rapidly shifting political scene in France at that time. During the Hundred Days in 1815 when Napoleon escaped and Lazare Carnot was in the political power structure again, Sadi was disgusted to find that his humble junior-lieutenant's room was visited by high-ranking officers anxious to curry favor with the son of Lazare. Shortly, the monarchy was restored, Lazare exiled, and Sadi was posted to a remote garrison far from Paris, doing the most routine jobs. In

1820 at age twenty-four he retired on half-pay and moved to Paris.

Sadi then entered the most creative period of his life, studying widely at the Sorbonne, the Collège de France, and the École des Mines, concentrating mostly on physics and economics. He spent a lot of time visiting factories and studying the organization and economics of various industries. His diligence and quick mind soon made him an expert on the industries of different countries of Europe. One remaining fragment of his economic writings demonstrates that his economic ideas were even further advanced than his thermodynamic ideas; he envisaged the use of taxes not merely as a source of revenue but also as a means of guiding the agricultural and industrial development of the country.

After Lazare died in exile in 1823, Hippolyte, Sadi's younger brother, returned to Paris where he and Sadi set up a small apartment. It was here that Sadi wrote *Reflections on the Motive Power of Fire*. He made Hippolyte read parts of the manuscript to make sure that the treatise would be intelligible to the nonscientist. In this short book he examined several different types of engines, both steam- and air-operated. But the importance of his work was that Carnot transcended the technical details of specific engines and examined the fundamental rules governing the conversion of heat to work and thereby took the first and largest step in establishing what we now call the second law of thermodynamics.

Sadi's memoir was published in 1824 and sold for three francs. It received one long, excellent review, but scarcely anyone bought the book and a few years later it was out of print.

In 1832 Sadi caught scarlet fever but recovered. While convalescing in the country, he contracted cholera and died at age thirty-six. Except for some attention from Émile Clapeyron, the second law lay dormant for some twenty-five years until Rudolf J. Clausius and William Thomson (Lord Kelvin) clearly formulated it without reference to caloric theory and began to apply it systematically.

The heat was oppressive. A less determined man of smaller vision would have rested in his bunk. Julius Robert Mayer, ship's doctor on the *Java*, a three-masted schooner 100 days out of Rotterdam on the way to Surabaja, was not such a man. Mayer, but twenty-seven years old in the year 1840, on the long voyage out read Antoine Lavoisier's work on chemistry and was fascinated by the ideas presented there.

Lavoisier said that animal heat results from the slow combustion of food. Mayer thought about this idea and tried to connect it with his medical studies in which he had learned that the blood of the arteries was bright, while the blood of the veins was dark. When they reached Surabaja, twenty-eight sailors had come down with fever. As Mayer was bleeding them, he noted how bright the venous blood was; it was almost as bright as the arterial blood he had seen in medical school in Germany. It appeared that this bright red blood was full of oxygen—that it had not been "burnt" as completely as that from people in more northern climates.

Could it be that the body need not expend as much energy in maintaining its temperature in the tropics as in Germany? Mayer stayed on board when the other crew members got off to explore the islands of the Indies. He wanted to organize what he had seen; he wanted to reduce his observations to law. He wanted to show that, in general, there is a relation, even an equivalence, between work and heat. In short, he wanted to show that energy is conserved.

While it is true that Rumford had arrived at a correct understanding of the nature of heat, he did not fully appreciate the quantitative relation between the mechanical work expended and the heat produced. Mayer, however, was ready in 1842 to generalize what he had observed on board ship and state unequivocally: "A force once in existence cannot be annihilated." Mayer consistently used the word *force* where we now use the word *energy*. Since *force* had been given another meaning by Newton, some ambiguity resulted from this misnomer. In the terminology we use today Mayer observed that whenever one kind of energy disappears another kind always appears to take its place.

Mayer's ideas had tough sledding: the established physicists of the day ignored them and the local townspeople and press ridiculed them. His beliefs were in conflict with accepted doctrine and he presented them in difficult language. If this lack of acceptance were not enough, he had the misfortune to see all his discoveries made elsewhere by others and credited to them. In 1843 and following years Joule investigated the convertibility of work and heat and measured the mechanical equivalent of heat. Many of Joule's statements parallel those of Mayer. In 1847 Helmholtz independently discovered and clearly set forth the principle of conservation of energy and applied it to several branches of physics. There was scarcely a thing that Mayer wrote that someone else did not write later and receive praise for.

To a certain extent Mayer's lack of recognition was his own fault. It was, of course, not his fault that reputable journals would not publish his articles. But who would expect to find one of the great generalizations of science, the first law of thermodynamics, in a privately printed pamphlet on nutrition written by a small-town physician?

The cumulative scorn and ridicule poured on him, coupled with praise for his contemporaries when they came forth with things he had already discovered, took their toll. He grew more and more frantic and found it nearly impossible to sleep. One night in 1850 his agitation grew so great that he threw himself out of a window to the paved street two stories below. The fall did not kill him but added considerable physical suffering to his mental anguish. In 1851 he was committed to an asylum where he was abused and tormented. He was released two years later but never fully regained his health.

In 1862, John Tyndall, an eminently fair-minded scientist, delivered a lecture entitled "On Force," at the Royal Institution

(Rumford's old homestead). He acknowledged Mayer's contributions and called the world's attention to the significance of Mayer's work. Prior to Tyndall's accolades only Clausius in Germany had supported Mayer's achievements. It has been said many times that no man is a prophet in his own land. That adage is nowhere proved to be more true than in this case. Mayer's recognition in England immediately spread to Germany where high honors were bestowed upon him by governments and learned societies.

The man who had been ignored by his colleagues, ridiculed by his neighbors, abused in an asylum, and even reported dead by vicious gossip, finally received the recognition so long denied him. His latter years were days of rest, peace, and recognition. The King of Württemberg ennobled him and he was awarded the Poncelet Prize. In 1871 the Royal Society presented him with their highest honor, the Copley Medal, a year after they presented the same award to Joule. Tyndall gave the address on both occasions. Death came to him peacefully at the age of sixty-four in 1878.

Hermann von Helmholtz (1821–1894) was a German philosopher and man of science with many interests. Because his parents were poor, they felt they could not afford to let him follow a purely scientific career and he thus became a surgeon in the Prussian army.

Later he taught physiology and anatomy in several German universities. In connection with his physiological studies of the eye he invented the ophthalmoscope in order to examine the interior of the eye and another device for measurement of the curvature of the eye. He also studied the ear and hearing and advanced the theory that differences in pitch are detected through the action of the cochlea, a spiral organ in the inner ear. He analyzed musical tones, deducing that combinations of notes sounded well or discordant on the basis of wavelengths and the production of beats at particular rates. Since he was an accomplished musician, he must have enjoyed his application of science to the art of music.

We cite him here because of his clear formulation of the principle of conservation of energy, a study he was led to by his investigations of muscle action. He was the first to show that animal heat is produced chiefly by contracting muscle and that an acid (today we know it to be lactic acid) is formed in the working muscle.

Though Mayer first postulated the conservation of energy in 1842, Helmholtz did it independently with much greater clarity and detail in 1847. However, the same journal that rejected Mayer's work also rejected Helmholtz's and he too had his paper privately printed.

Helmholtz used his conservation ideas to oppose those scientists who believed there was a unique "vital force" in living organisms. He reasoned that living organisms containing such a "force" could be perpetual motion machines—which they are not.

Since Helmholtz worked in hydrodynamics, electrodynamics, and meteorological physics as well as thermodynamics and physiology, he rivaled Faraday as a nearly universal scientist. Furthermore, Helmholtz wrote as an empiricist on philosophical and aesthetic topics.

William Thomson (no relation to Benjamin Thompson) was a creative yet rigid individual. When he was near the age of sixty, toward the end of the nineteenth century, he declared that *all* of the discoveries in physics had been made and that all that remained to be done was to adjust the last few decimal places in the various physical constants. Nevertheless, Thomson's contributions to thermodynamics were considerable and he is justly honored for them. In 1892 he was raised to the peerage, whereupon he took the title Lord Kelvin.

In 1835 at age eleven he entered the University of Glasgow where he finished second in his class in mathematics. He wrote his first paper on mathematics when he was still in his teens; a professor read it to the Royal Society of Edinburgh so it would not seem that so prestigious an institution was being lectured by a schoolboy.

Thomson was interested in heat and he collaborated with Joule to develop a method to cool a gas by expanding it. This phenomenon, called the Joule-Thomson effect, played a prime role a generation later in the development of techniques for liquefying gases.

He also explored the consequences of the fact that the volumes of many gases are reduced by a factor of $\frac{1}{273}$ of their volumes at 0°C (degrees Centigrade) for every drop in temperature of 1°C. In 1848 he suggested that the energy of motion of molecules reached zero at minus 273°C and later concluded that there must be an absolute zero of temperature, a temperature below which no temperature can exist. He proposed an absolute temperature scale based on this notion (now called the Kelvin scale in his honor) and it is used today throughout the scientific world.

In the 1860's Thomson turned his attention to the construction of the Atlantic cable, becoming chief electrician on the cable-laying ship, the *Great Eastern*. He improved the cable and developed the galvanometer used to detect the faint signals that the first cable carried. He was knighted because of this work.

Kelvin died in 1907. His life had spanned the technological gap between the first steam locomotive and the first airplane. He had made important theoretical and practical contributions to the scientific and technological advances of his time.

A student approached his professor in his office and asked him to go over a diagram the professor had explained in class. The professor began to draw imaginary lines across the floor; the lines grew more complicated—going up the walls, along the ceiling, and then across the door. As the confused student left the office, he turned and saw his professor, Josiah Willard Gibbs, standing in the center of the floor completely absorbed in his diagram.

Willard Gibbs, named after his father who was a Hebrew scholar and Professor of Sacred Literature at Yale University, was born the year before Robert Mayer set sail for Java. His achievements in a wide range of scientific areas cause him to be acknowledged today throughout the world as one of the greatest American-born scientists.

Now everyone tries to claim Willard Gibbs for their own, though when he was alive he was little known and rather taken for granted by most of those who did know him. Mechanical engineers claim him to be theirs since his thesis topic at Yale was entitled "On the Form of the Teeth of Wheels in Spur Gearing." Mathematicians say he was surely of their kind since in the years between 1881 and 1884 he developed the subject of vector analysis. Physicists claim Gibbs for his development of statistical mechanics, which he applied to largely thermodynamical problems. Chemists honor Gibbs because of his pioneering work on the application of thermodynamics to chemistry. He did all these things with a modesty that was almost an obsession with him. He described his own work and attitude simply by stating: "Anyone with the same desires could have made the same researches." Like Mayer, Gibbs came to be recognized largely after scientific leaders in other countries appreciated the importance of his work. For Gibbs it was no less a scientist than James Clerk Maxwell of the Cavendish Laboratory who first recognized the great value of his theoretical discoveries.

Gibbs, in his first two papers in 1873, extended the work of earlier thermodynamicists by tying together in a logical way the energy and entropy of a system with its pressure, temperature, and volume. He also developed a graphical method to show by means of a surface, rather than a plane as was customary, the interrelationship of three variables such as energy, entropy, and volume. In Gibbs's masterpiece, "The Equilibrium of Heterogenous Substances," he set forth a complete and exhaustive study of equilibrium between two or more components in a single system. In this same paper he gives his discovery of the chemical potential, considered by many to be his greatest contribution to science. The chemical potential is a principal link between thermodynamics and physical chemistry.

Gibbs used models to illustrate his work, but his models were mathematical ones. Maxwell went one step further; he took the mathematical description of the properties of water that Gibbs had proposed in one of his papers and had several plaster surfaces or statues made to fit the description. He sent one to Gibbs and kept two others at the Cavendish Laboratory. The story quickly spread among the students at Yale that Maxwell had sent the unusual gift to Professor Gibbs. One student is said to have asked Gibbs who sent him the model. Gibbs answered, "A friend sent it to me." The student, knowing full well the answer, asked "Who is the friend?" But Gibbs, encumbered by the modesty that was an innate part of his life, only answered: "A friend in England."

In 1880 the president of Johns Hopkins University approached Gibbs and offered him an attractive position at the school in Baltimore, which was then only four years old. Gibbs was greatly flattered even though he felt himself to be an integral part of Yale. After much thought he decided to accept the offer, but before sending off his letter of acceptance a friend of his informed the president of Yale of Gibbs's planned departure. Yale was not to be raided so easily—they decided to start paying their Professor of Mathematical Physics, something they had neglected to do since his appointment to the post in 1871. Gibbs did not leave New Haven. The next year Gibbs was awarded the Rumford Medal by the American Academy of Arts and Science.

Part of the explosive growth of the chemical industry in the past forty years is directly traceable to the work that Gibbs did before the turn of the century. Though his interest in practical things disappeared shortly after he took out a successful patent on a railroad brake in 1866, Gibbs has influenced some of the world's greatest industries in ways even he never dreamed possible.

In 1903 Gibbs died after a short illness. He was buried in the Grove Street Cemetery in New Haven near his rock, Yale.

We now turn our attention to some of the contemporary workers in thermodynamics.

One of the men who has followed in the footsteps of Gibbs is Lars Onsager, born in Norway in 1903, who is now the J. Willard Gibbs Professor of Theoretical Chemistry at Yale. After being appointed Sterling Fellow in Chemistry at Yale in 1933 for his contributions to the theory of electrolyte solutions, the Chemistry Department was surprised to discover that they had awarded a postdoctoral fellowship to a man who did not have a doctorate. They suggested that for the record he present his current work as a thesis. They were even more surprised by his dissertation of over 100 pages on the properties of a special mathematical function; it was hardly a conventional topic for a chemistry thesis. The mathematicians at Yale came to the rescue by agreeing that the dissertation was an outstanding contribution to their subject.

Several of Onsager's important scientific contributions have not been published in the usual ways. On one occasion he wrote the solution to a fundamental problem on a blackboard following a lecture by the physicist (and thermodynamicist) L. Tisza. Some of his other major contributions have appeared either as discussions following other people's papers or only as printed abstracts of papers presented orally at meetings.

Onsager has contributed to many areas of chemistry, mathematics, and physics; we cite him here because of his fundamental contributions to irreversible thermodynamics—a subject we shall touch on briefly a little later. He has recived numerous awards for his work, including the Rumford Gold Medal.

William Francis Giauque, a physical chemist at the University of California, received the Nobel Prize in chemistry in 1949 for his work in thermodynamics. He (along with Peter J. W. Debye, who did the same thing independently and nearly simultaneously) first proposed the idea of the adiabatic demagnetization method of reaching temperatures below those that can be reached with liquid helium, which boils at −269°C. A few years later he reduced his theory to practice and made his method work. He also was one of the principals who helped establish the third law of thermodynamics. Giauque was one of the first to work out and successfully apply the principles (Gibbsian, in part) of statistical mechanics to calculating the thermodynamic properties of gases. He also discovered the isotopes of oxygen in his spare time. Giauque is a serious, imposing man, but not without humor, as indicated by this passage written with Brodale, Fisher, and Hornung in the *Journal of Chemical Physics* (1965).

The word "point" is an old and formerly respected term in thermodynamics. Recently there has been a rapidly growing downgrading of this accurate word in connection with various phenomena which are obviously gradual in nature. There is undoubtedly a real requirement for some brief way in which to refer to approximate temperatures in connection with gradual transitions. The Greeks probably did not have a name for this one, but there is a substandard English which seems sufficiently imprecise to cover such indefinite situations. We refer to the vernacular in which oil is "erl" and pearl is "poil." From this dialect we have mined the word "pernt," which seems loose enough to cover the approximate temperature range of gradual effects.

Scientists who are at least reputed to favor accuracy of thought and expression should welcome an elastic substitute for the word point, which would allow its return to its proper

status. . . . This is illiterally a Pernt of Order and Disorder,
for those who do not mind stretching a point. . . .

We take it as some small sign of improvement in the human
condition that humor and rational arguments are increasingly
more common than polemics in current scientific discussions.

Peter J. W. Debye is a Dutch-born scientist who, though his
original training was in electrical engineering, turned to physics
and then physical chemistry. He succeeded Einstein as professor
of theoretical physics in Zurich in 1911. Much of Debye's early
work combined application of thermodynamics, quantum theory,
and statistical mechanics to solids. He also made important contributions to the study of crystal structure by means of X-ray
scattering and to the electric properties of matter. 'Lately he has
done important work on polymers.

One of Debye's most important contributions was the extension
and correction of Svante Arrhenius' work on the nature of solutions of salts, called electrolyte solutions. Arrhenius had presented
convincing evidence that many substances in solution yield
charged particles called ions. From electrical conductivities and
freezing points of such solutions he had deduced that some of the
dissolved "molecules" were split up into ions while others in the
same solution remained in the neutral "molecular" state. He treated
this problem in much the same manner as is now used for a variety
of chemical equilibria, as discussed later in this book. Arrhenius'
idea was very successful when applied to such slightly ionized
substances as acetic acid, but was open to serious criticism when
applied to salts such as sodium chloride. Debye and Hückel resolved this problem with a paper published in 1923 in which they
showed that sodium chloride and similar dissolved substances are
entirely in the form of ions and that the previously disconcerting
behavior could be accounted for by a clever combination of
thermodynamics with electrostatics and statistics. This one paper

virtually revolutionized the study of many solutions of chemical importance.

Because of the political situation in Germany, Debye came to Cornell University in the United States in 1940, just four years after his achievements had been recognized by the award of the Nobel Prize in chemistry.

Although Linus Pauling has not been primarily a thermodynamicist, he has made important use of thermodynamic data in his work on molecular structure and the nature of the chemical bond, leading to the Nobel Prize in chemistry in 1954. In his spare time, he worked vigorously enough in the cause of peace to gain a second Nobel Prize in 1962 and lots of enemies that any man of good will could be proud of.

Gilbert Newton Lewis (highly appropriate given names for a scientist) was an American chemist who got his start in chemical research under Theodore William Richards at Harvard. This early research by Lewis and Richards was one of the first clues leading to the third law of thermodynamics. After short stays in Europe, the Massachusetts Institute of Technology, and the Philippines, he went to the University of California in 1912, where he was chiefly responsible for founding a tremendously productive school of chemistry that was for many years largely devoted to chemical applications of thermodynamics. Nobel Prize winners Urey, Giauque, Seaborg, Calvin, and Libby all studied in his department, and Pauling has often acknowledged his scientific indebtedness to Lewis. Others among Lewis' scientific descendants and their descendants unto several generations are still among the leaders in thermodynamics. In addition to Lewis' direct influence on so many first-rate scientists, in 1923 he and Randall published a book on chemical thermodynamics that may well be the world's most quoted scientific book.

Lewis was one of the first to recognize the great value of Gibbs's work. He contributed importantly in transforming the general but obscure equations of Gibbs into more specific and directly useful equations that could be applied to a variety of problems. Lewis, partly through his book with Randall, can therefore be regarded as a principal popularizer of Gibbs. Lewis also developed important new ideas in the applications of thermodynamics to many problems and was an ingenious inventor of new experimental approaches.

Lewis was a knowledgeable man of high principles and strongly held views on many subjects. In addition to his work in thermodynamics, he did important research on the theory of chemical binding, on the colors and optical properties of organic substances, on the isotopes of hydrogen, and wrote on such diverse subjects as economics and the philosophy of science.

As the size and complexity of our society grows, so grow the demands on our network of communications. We as individuals want to talk by telephone more frequently to more people who are farther away. Industrial complexes that are guided in their operations to an increasing extent by computers require more information from more distant points than ever before. Television networks wish to distribute more television programs to more places.

Claude Shannon, born in 1916, is a mathematician who has studied messages and the most efficient way to send them. His work has led to a method of expressing quantitatively the amount of information in a message so that the likelihood of losing information by garbling, distortion, or other means can be predicted. This branch of science is called information theory and several of the concepts of thermodynamics, notably those associated with entropy, can be shown to be analogous to similar concepts in information theory. Since entropy, of which we shall tell more later, is a measure of disorder, it is easy to see that it may be related to the order and disorder of messages.

E. T. Jaynes went still further in 1957 when he showed that if one assumes that the ideas of information theory are more basic than those of thermodynamics, all the formulae of statistical mechanics can be derived from them. Once the statistical mechanic formulae are obtained, the laws of thermodynamics can then be derived. This was quite an accomplishment, since "laws" of nature are normally not considered to be derivable; they are taken as correct or true because we do not observe violations of them. If one accepts Jaynes's derivations, then one accepts his hypothesis that the concepts of information theory are more fundamental than the concepts of thermodynamics. This has led to, and will continue to provoke, some interesting "discussions."

We have begun our tale with some of the highlights from the lives of men who have made thermodynamics what it is today—a vital, viable branch of science and engineering that offers us keen insight into the world around us. We think you will find the science of thermodynamics as interesting as the scientists who have made it. Read on!

chapter two
temperature

Without doubt man's first instrument for sensing hot and cold was his hand. When we touch an object, we employ our *temperature sense* to attribute to the object a property called *temperature*. The hotter it feels, the higher the temperature. In many respects this procedure plays the same role in qualitative science that lifting an object does in determining its weight. Temperature now has numbers associated with it and indicates quantitatively how hot or cold an object is.

The concept of temperature has been bound up with two considerations that have always been with man: his health and the weather. Plutarch (A.D. 46–120) commented on the former in *Demetrius* thus:

> Once Antigonus was told his son was ill and went to see him. At the door he met some young beauty. Going in, he sat down by the bed and took his pulse. "The fever," said Demetrius, "has just left me." "Oh yes," replied his father, "I met it going out the door."

Galen, a physician who lived in the second century, based his patients' treatment to a large extent on the theory that individual differences, whether of sickness or health, or in body habits, or racial origins, were in fact differences in the proportions of the four qualities: heat, cold, moisture, and dryness. The "complexion" of a person was determined by the proportion in which these qualities were tempered, and that is where we get the word *temperament*, which has not drifted far from its original meaning, and *temperature*, which has today a very precise physical meaning. But Galen's chief contribution to thermometry was his description of temperature by numbers. It is interesting to note that the physician Galen applied his ideas to the drugs that had the power of heating or cooling a patient. Thus poppies were judged to be cold because of their stupefying effect. His organizational bent was so great that he classified drugs as hot or cold in the first, second, third, or fourth degree.

In 1578, twenty-five years before the invention of the thermometer, Joannes Haslerus, another physician, suggested the notion of a *temperature scale;* he put forth this idea in a treatise largely devoted to calculations intended to show the degree of heating or cooling effectiveness possessed by mixtures of several drugs.

It was just after the beginning of the seventeenth century that several scientific workers came upon the idea of measuring temperature by means of a device which is now seen to resemble in some ways an ordinary weather thermometer. Their instruments were derived from an experiment carried out by Philo of Byzantium in the third century B.C. His experiment with a hollow glass globe sealed to one end of a glass tube dipping into water showed that air expands when heated and contracts when cooled. This simple demonstration of the expansive property of air was repeated with numerous ingenious modifications by Hero of Alexandria, who credits Philo as the originator of the experiment.

Galileo Galilei had good friends. Although he is usually credited with the invention of the first instrument which we could call a thermometer, his claim rests mainly on the testimony of his friends and pupils; his own surviving writings seem to contain only one incidental reference to the instrument. Galileo's instrument should really be called a "barothermoscope," as in its early form it lacked a definite scale and the readings it yielded were very much dependent on atmospheric pressure.

Galileo's instrument used a glass sphere about the size of a hen's egg and an arrangement similar to that employed by Philo, as shown in Figure 2–1. As the glass ball was warmed by the hand or any other object whose temperature was to be measured, the air was driven out as it expanded. When the hand or hot object was removed, the air inside cooled and contracted, allowing the water to rise in the tube. The level to which the water rose in the tube was a rough indication of the extent to which the air had been heated. Galileo's invention is believed to have occurred sometime during the period between 1592 and 1603. Several other scientists, including Santorio, Fludd, and Drebbel, worked independently on similar devices about the same time. In 1611 Santorio gave the first written record of the invention.

Figure 2–1
Fludd's air thermometer as drawn in his *Meteorologica Cosmica* published in 1626. This device is very similar to Galileo's thermoscope. Fludd recommended that the lower part be enclosed in a wooden box so that no one would be able to see how it worked. It is filled with a solution of blue vitriol to prevent freezing and also to render the liquid more visible.

In 1632 another physician, Jean Rey, made a significant improvement in Galileo's instrument when he used water as the working fluid in the thermometer instead of air. By 1654 the Grand Duke Ferdinand II of Tuscany had substituted colored alcohol [1] for water and was the first to seal both ends of his in-

_____

[1] *It is unauthoritatively rumored that Ferdinand II had to give up his researches in this area because no matter how much colored alcohol he brought into the laboratory, he rarely had enough around when he wanted to conduct an experiment. He noted in his laboratory notebook that the evaporation rate of colored alco-*

strument. Divisions on these thermometers were made directly on the glass stem. The only attempt made by the Florentine Academy to secure fixed points for comparison of thermometers consisted in taking the lowest position the alcohol registered in Tuscany in mid-winter and the highest point registered in mid-summer. These points coincided approximately with the sixteenth and the eightieth divisions on the hundred division thermometer. Figure 2–2 illustrates two Florentine thermometers.

 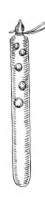

Figure 2–2
Thermometers developed in the Florentine Accademia del Cimento (Academy of Experiments) in the middle of the seventeenth century. The thermometer on the left shows the glass-blowing skills of the members of the academy. The thermometer on the right used a number of glass bubbles suspended in alcohol, their weight being adjusted so that first one and then another would sink as the temperature rose and the density of the alcohol decreased.

Isaac Newton was not one to let an interesting area of science slip by without his making a contribution. In 1701 he published anonymously a paper that gave a temperature scale ranging from the freezing point of water (0° Newton) to the heat of "coals in a little kitchen fire made from bituminous coal and excited by the use of a bellows" (192° Newton). He also gave intermediate points such as the temperatures required to boil water and melt wax. In the course of his paper he also proposed the law of cool-

hol was very high, even in tightly stoppered bottles. He never, so far as is known, established any correlation between the high evaporation rate and the good-natured incompetence of his assistants in afternoon laboratory sessions.

ing that bears his name today. This law stated that the rate at which a body will cool at any moment is in proportion to the excess of its temperature above that of its surroundings. This law is now known to hold only for small temperature differences, but at the time it was a significant contribution to the infant science of heat.

Our common measures of time and angles in terms of hours, minutes, seconds, and degrees are derived from the ancient Sumerians of the Mesopotamian Valley who made use of a sexagesimal system of numeration. It is not as obvious, but nevertheless true, that the common measure of temperature in terms of degrees Fahrenheit is likewise a product of Sumerian or Babylonian influence. Very early in the eighteenth century Ole Römer, a Danish astronomer, carried out investigations in thermometry in which he chose the boiling point of water as his higher fixed point and the temperature of a mixture of ice, salt, and water as the lower fixed point. It then remained to divide the interval between these points in some "rational" manner. What could have been more rational to an astronomer than to follow the traditional usage of the Babylonians in astronomy and continued in Greek, Arabic, and Latin works which used the sexagesimal subdivisions? In view of this tradition, it seems natural that Römer should have adopted sixty divisions for his thermometer. His lowest and highest temperatures became 0 and 60, respectively. Römer noted that water froze at about 7½ or 8 degrees and that normal body temperature was approximately 22½ degrees on his thermometer.

In 1708 Gabriel Daniel Fahrenheit visited Römer in Copenhagen and found him busy calibrating thermometers. Observing Römer's work, he was led to adopt the same fundamental principles in his own work with some minor changes. Fahrenheit chose the same lower fixed point but elected to take body temperature as his upper reference point. He found Römer's scale too coarse, so he divided each of the sixty subdivisions into four parts. The freezing point of water thus became $4 \times 8 = 32$ and the body temperature

$4 \times 22\frac{1}{2} = 90$. Later he changed the scale slightly so that normal body temperature would correspond to 96 instead of 90; on this modified scale he found that water boiled at 212 rather than 240, thus yielding 180 degrees between the freezing and boiling points of water. "Fahrenheit" thermometers today are calibrated on the basis of the freezing and boiling points of water, so that Fahrenheit's upper fixed point, body temperature, is now only an incidental intermediate point at 98.6. No doubt, the modifications made on the original scale have served to hide the origins of the Fahrenheit temperature scale.

The origins of a thermometer scale with 100 subdivisions between the freezing and boiling points of water are not so clear. The first suggestion may have been in 1710 by a Swede named Elvius. The centigrade system is often credited to Anders Celsius, a Swedish astronomer, possibly because of a casual association suggested by the "C" for centigrade, coupled with the fact that Celsius used a centesimal system as early as 1742. Celsius, not a man to be bound by tradition, no matter how logical, fixed the boiling point of water at 0 and the freezing point at 100. It is believed that he did this to avoid negative temperatures below the melting point of ice (apparently he was unconcerned about negative temperatures above the boiling point of water). A few years later an astronomer colleague of Celsius by the name of Marten Stromer reversed the fixed points and produced the centesimal scale we know and use today.

Guillaume Amontons was a French experimenter whose interest in thermometry stemmed from his work in meteorology. Amontons discovered in 1701 that the thermal expansion of air is surprisingly uniform. He noted that if a fixed volume of air at any initial pressure is heated from room temperature to the boiling point of water, the pressure in every case will increase by about one-third. He thus deduced that for equal changes in temperature the pressure of a constant volume of gas will be increased or decreased by the same fraction of the pressure at an arbitrary point. Amontons studied his observations carefully and then put forth two radical suggestions that were not accepted for many years.

Amontons was the first to conceive of an absolute scale of temperature, and also pointed out that only one fixed point is necessary. He chose the boiling point of water as his fixed point, with the temperature measured in terms of the proportionate increase or decrease in pressure of a given volume of air. He reported the following experimental results:

Observed pressure	Temperature of the
73 units	Boiling point of water
58 units	Greatest summer heat
51 or 52 units	Freezing point of water

At the time it was made, his next observation represented a very great radical departure from the then infant sciences of thermometry and heat. He proposed that by extrapolation below the freezing point of water it could be inferred that at some temperature, called absolute zero, the air in his thermometer would exert no pressure; he reasoned that it would have no elasticity because its parts would be contiguous and cease to move. Figure 2–3 illustrates the extrapolation process that Amontons proposed. His contemporaries were skeptical of his conclusions and his suggestion of an absolute thermometric scale lay dormant until the middle of the nineteenth century when Lord Kelvin (William Thomson) and Rudolf Clausius both set forth theories that pointed to the existence of absolute zero.

We conclude this discussion of temperature scales by mentioning the ones in general use today. We present four: the two scales whose origins we have discussed, Fahrenheit (F) and Celsius (C), and the two absolute scales associated with each of these, Rankine and Kelvin (K). In 1848 Lord Kelvin (who did not invent the Kelvinator) published a paper proposing an absolute temperature scale; however, the scale he proposed in that year

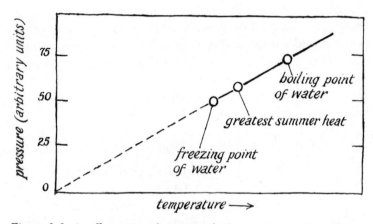

Figure 2–3. An illustration of Amontons' idea concerning the relation between temperature and the pressure of a given volume of air. He proposed that at some temperature which one might call absolute zero the air in his thermometer would exert zero pressure.

was unsatisfactory. A short time later (1851) he devised a temperature scale compatible with the first and second laws of thermodynamics—an achievement of no small stature.[2] The scale he proposed is in use today and locates absolute zero 273°C below the freezing point of water. The Rankine scale locates absolute zero 492°F below the freezing point of water. These four scales are compared in Figure 2–4.

In 1939 W. F. Giauque of the University of California renewed the earlier proposal made by Amontons and Lord Kelvin that one

[2] *Lord Kelvin certainly deserves all of the honors that have been bestowed on him, but perhaps just once a year we ought to have a Guillaume Amontons Day so that people the world over would remember that he was the fellow who first suggested the concept of an absolute zero of temperature and pointed out that you need but one fixed point to define a temperature scale.*

should simply define the temperature of a single fixed point. Giauque's proposal has subsequently been adopted by the International Unions of Physics and Chemistry. The fixed point that is now adopted is the triple point of water. The phase rule of Gibbs predicts and experiments verify that a pure substance can have its three phases (solid, liquid, and vapor) in equilibrium at only one temperature and one pressure. For water the triple point pressure is equivalent to a 4.58 millimeter column of mercury and the temperature is assigned the value 273.16°K. This value is chosen to maintain the traditional difference of 100.00°K between the boiling point of water (373.15°K) and the ordinary melting point of ice (273.15°K).

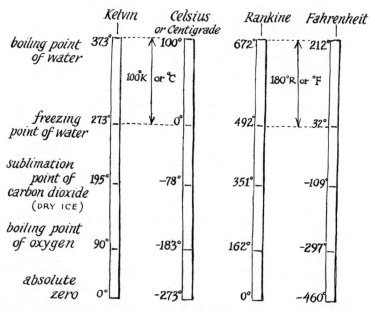

Figure 2–4. Comparison of the Kelvin, Celsius, Rankine, and Fahrenheit temperature scales. Temperatures have been rounded off to the nearest degree.

The triple point may be achieved by introducing very pure water into a cell like that shown in Figure 2–5. When all the air has been removed, the vessel is sealed and a freezing mixture is placed in the inner well. After some of the water is frozen the freezing mixture is replaced by a thermometer which melts a thin layer of

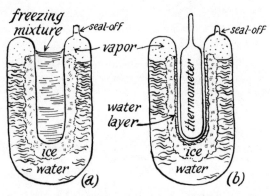

Figure 2–5. A schematic diagram of a triple point cell—
(a) with freezing mixture in the central well to freeze a layer of ice; (b) with a thermometer in the well, which melts a thin layer of ice around the inner well wall.

the ice around the wall. So long as the solid, liquid, and vapor phases coexist in equilibrium, the system is at the triple point.

Since scientists like to sneak up on a problem, they sometimes seem to propose laws which on first inspection appear trivial. The first general law of nature that we shall discuss in this book is called, appropriately enough, the *zeroth law of thermodynamics.* Imagine that we have two systems whose properties (such as pressure, density, temperature, etc.) are uniform throughout each system and note further that the values of these properties are not changing with time. The systems are thermally insulated from each other and also from their surroundings. The zeroth law is intended to answer the question, "Are these two systems at the same temperature?"

To determine whether they are at the same temperature, we remove the insulating material from a portion of each system and bring the exposed surfaces into contact. If no observable changes take place in the thermodynamic properties of either system, the two are at the same temperature. Assume that system C is at the same temperature as system A as determined by this test, and that C is at the same temperature as system B. Then by the same

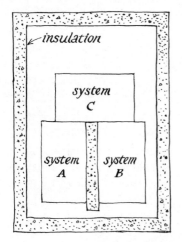 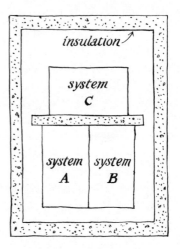

Figure 2–6. The zeroth law of thermodynamics.

test, systems A and B must be at the same temperature. This state of affairs is illustrated in Figure 2–6. More formally: *When two systems are at the same temperature as a third, they are at the same temperature as each other.* R. H. Fowler called this postulate the zeroth law of thermodynamics. This law clearly turns the thermometer into a useful instrument by eliminating the need for bringing into physical contact each pair of systems whose temperatures you wish to compare.

At first the zeroth law appears to be so obvious as to be trivial, but this is not so. Consider the following two analogies. An amber rod A that has been rubbed with fur will attract a pith ball C. So will another amber rod B, but the two amber rods will not attract each other. Or consider the plots of numerous modern novels, which may be summarized as follows: Abigail is in love with Cadwallader. Bernadette is in love with Cadwallader. But does Abigail love Bernadette?

Man can survive only in a very narrow range of temperatures. The physiological makeup of man ensures that his own body temperature remains within certain limits. Body temperatures in excess of 108°F or below 90°F are rarely encountered in adult clinical practice. One extreme example occurred in the recent past when a child suffering from severe exposure was brought into a hospital where her temperature was recorded as 60.8°F. Except for some frostbite, she made a complete recovery. It is interesting to note that lowering the body temperature to 68°F reduces the body's metabolism to 25 per cent of its normal rate. Surgeons have taken advantage of the resulting reduced load on the heart to carry out open-heart surgery. They have been able to perform some remarkable clear field surgery in the heart after the body temperature has been lowered to 86°F. The body can be kept at this temperature for as long as 8 minutes.

The temperature of man's environment does not span a very great range either. In 1922 in Azizia, Tripolitania, in North Africa, a temperature of 136°F was recorded under standard conditions (the thermometer is located in a louvered box which permits free circulation of air). At the other extreme, researchers at the Soviet Antarctic station of Vostok recorded a temperature of −126.9°F in August, 1960.

What range of temperature does man encounter in his universe? The range is indeed many times greater than the narrow span in which he can survive. An illustration of the extent of the known

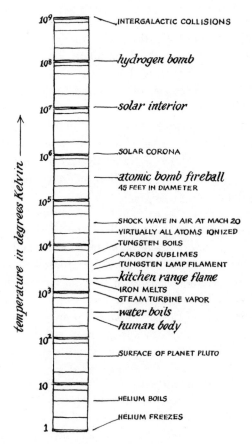

Figure 2–7. Range of temperatures.

range of temperatures is shown in Figure 2–7. It extends from the low end of about 0.000001°K to a high temperature in excess of 1,000,000,000°K—close to the interior temperature of the hottest star. Man himself has produced temperatures near 10^8 degrees K [3]

[3] *Scientists find it convenient to write very large numbers by using exponents to signify how many times ten is multiplied by itself or,*

in the hydrogen bomb reaction. Man can survive over only about one-millionth of one-millionth of the range from 10^{-6} to 10^8 degrees K that he has been able to produce.

What are the techniques used today to measure this range of temperature? It is obvious that the gas and liquid thermometers of Amontons and Rey do not possess the flexibility or range required by today's varied technology. Because the number of techniques is so large, we can only mention a few of the devices in current use. We have chosen to describe some devices because they have found wide application and others because they illustrate an interesting principle.

Every thermometer has a *thermometric property*. The zeroth law of thermodynamics provides that the reading of the thermometer is the temperature of *all* systems in thermal equilibrium with it. The properties that we desire in a thermometer are *sensitivity*—an appreciable change in the thermometric property produced by a relatively small change in temperature; *accuracy* in the measurement of the thermometric property so that its readings compare favorably with agreed-upon standards; *reproducibility* so that results can be duplicated consistently; and *speed* in

---

in the case of a small number, how many times ten is divided into one. For example, the number 1,000,000,000 is conveniently written 1×10^9, which means $10 \times 10 \times 10 \times 10 \times 10 \times 10 \times 10 \times 10 \times 10 = 1,000,000,000$. We see that the exponent 9 in this case tells us how many zeros follow the 1. We may write 0.000001 simply as 10^{-6}, since

$$10^{-6} = \frac{1}{10 \times 10 \times 10 \times 10 \times 10 \times 10} = 0.000001$$

A particular number may be written as follows, using the times sign ($\times$) to signify multiplication:

$$2.46 \times 10^4 \ (meaning \ 24{,}600)$$

$$6.5 \times 10^{-3} \ (meaning \ 0.0065)$$

coming into thermal equilibrium with the system whose temperature it is measuring.

As you step out on the porch to read the thermometer hanging on the wall, what you are looking at is the length of a column of colored alcohol confined in a bulb and very small tube called a capillary. This arrangement makes small changes in volume easily visible, and thus permits the small volume change that accompanies a change in temperature to be a useful thermometric property. The range of such liquid in glass thermometers is obviously limited on the low end by the freezing point of the liquid and on the high end by the pressure that builds up which can burst the glass. By using organic liquids that freeze at very low temperatures it is possible to construct liquid in glass thermometers that are useful at temperatures lower than $-100°$C. Mercury in glass thermometers commonly go to $360°$C and can be used as high as $600°$C. Gallium in quartz thermometers have been used to above $1000°$C.

As we have noted earlier, Amontons in 1701 observed that the pressure of a gas whose volume is kept constant is an excellent index to temperature; in fact, the modern constant volume gas thermometer has been accepted by bureaus of standards and university research laboratories the world over as *the* reference thermometer. A schematic of such a thermometer is illustrated in Figure 2–8. The gas, usually helium, is contained in bulb B which is connected to a mercury column C through a capillary tube. The volume of the gas is kept constant by adjusting the height of the mercury column C until the mercury just touches the tip of the projection of the capillary into the space above the mercury column known as the "nuisance volume." The height of the mercury column C is adjusted by raising or lowering the tube C'. The difference in height h between the two mercury columns C' and C is measured when the gas bulb B is surrounded by the system whose temperature is to be measured. The pressure of the gas contained in bulb B is given by the sum of the atmospheric pressure (in millimeters of mercury) and the height of column h. While the constant volume gas thermometer is regarded as a primary standard of temperature, it has several disadvantages. These thermometers are difficult to use for accurate work, are of awkward construction so that they do not fit into all environments, and attain thermal equilibrium slowly. Because of these difficulties, gas thermometers are used primarily in calibrating other thermometers that offer many advantages but do not have a thermometric property that is directly related to the thermodynamic temperature scale.

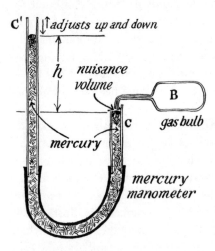

Figure 2–8
A constant volume gas thermometer. The gas bulb is located in the region where the temperature is to be measured. The height of the mercury column, h, is adjustable to keep the volume of the gas constant; it is proportional to the absolute temperature.

Aside from liquid in glass thermometers, thermocouples are probably the most widely used temperature measuring devices. When the ends of two dissimilar materials (metal wires in the case of temperature measurement) are joined together as shown in Figure 2–9 and the junctions of the wires are maintained at different temperatures, a voltage will appear across the other ends of the wires. This voltage is proportional to the difference between the temperatures of the junctions. This interesting effect was discovered in 1821 by Thomas Johann Seebeck, who reported that a magnetic needle is deflected when held near a circuit made of two different materials with a temperature gradient imposed on it. He attributed the deflection solely to the presence of the temperature difference and disregarded completely the current flowing in the circuit. Furthermore, he attempted to explain terrestrial magnetism as being caused by the temperature difference between the poles and the equator. Some of Seebeck's contempo-

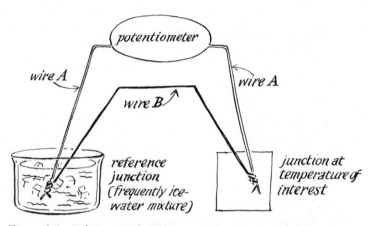

Figure 2–9. A thermocouple circuit made up of two different materials A and B. The reference junction is usually maintained at the temperature of melting ice. Thermocouples made with one leg of copper or iron and another of constantan (an alloy of copper and nickel) are frequently employed. Thermocouples with one leg of pure platinum and the other of 90 per cent platinum and 10 per cent rhodium are also used.

raries recognized that a current was induced in the circuit by the temperature difference and that it was this current that caused the magnetic needle to be deflected. Seebeck wasted a good many years trying to convince them that they were wrong.

For many purposes, the most convenient and precise temperature measurements are those made with resistance thermometers. As the name implies, these thermometers are based on the variation of electrical resistance with temperature. Useful secondary standard resistance thermometers are commonly made of fine platinum wire wound on a thin frame so constructed as to avoid strains in the wire when the temperature changes. In recent years, nickel resistance thermometers have come into use, largely because of the relatively large change of resistance per degree change in temperature. Developments in semiconductors that have contributed so much to electronics have also contributed importantly to resistance thermometry. Semiconductors called thermistors are now widely used as resistance thermometers. These materials have increasing resistance as the temperature decreases, in contrast with the opposite behavior of metals. But more importantly, the change of resistance with temperature is much larger than for metals, thus making thermistors very sensitive. Unfortunately, thermistors are less stable than metal resistance thermometers and require considerable care in their handling and frequent calibration when highly accurate results are needed.

Another interesting technique used to measure temperature is associated with the resonance oscillations of atoms about their equilibrium positions in a solid. Thermometers based on the principle of measuring the resonance frequency have been found to be very sensitive in the range from $10°$ to $300°K$. Quartz crystal thermometers that operate on this principle are commercially available and are finding increasing use.

What does a cocktail party have in common wtih a thermometer? The answer is *noise* if we are considering a rather special thermometer. Noise in the technical sense implies a random chaotic disturbance that is usually, like its ordinary cousin, unwanted. Electronic engineers generally design amplifiers and architects should always design rooms where people eat and drink so that the noise is minimal.

The random disturbances set up by the thermally excited vibrations of the atoms in a solid generate a voltage that is proportional to the absolute temperature and the impedance of the solid if it were located in a passive circuit. The impedance of a circuit element is analogous to its resistance except that it includes the effect of the inductance and capacitance of the circuit element. J. B. Garrison and A. W. Lanson in 1949 proposed a thermometer to make use of this phenomenon. It employed two resistors, one of which constituted the sensing probe, with the other so constructed that its impedance could be adjusted to generate the same noise voltage as the sensing resistor while being maintained at a reference temperature. Under these conditions there is a particularly simple relation between the two resistors' temperatures and impedances.

Such devices are independent of the material or the material's past history and may be employed over a wide range of conditions. Unfortunately, noise thermometers come to equilibrium slowly and require careful shielding to keep unwanted noise out of the complicated circuitry. While noise thermometers have not taken an important place in our technology, their development shows that even undesirable characteristics can be employed as thermometric properties.

All objects emit electromagnetic radiation whose intensity and frequency is closely related to the object's temperature. The equations used to describe these relationships were developed around the turn of the century; they are Planck's equation, the Stefan-Boltzmann equation, and Wien's displacement equation. The main advantages of using radiation to measure an object's temperature (called pyrometry) over other methods of temperature measurement are that: (1) the observer need only sight the pyrometer on the hot object; (2) the response is rapid; and (3) no lead wires or other physical connections with the system are required. Quantitative pyrometric temperature measurement methods are now highly developed, and can be used to measure temperatures from a few hundred degrees to several thousands of degrees Kelvin.

Figure 2–10 shows what was without a doubt the first optical pyrometer. A hot object barely glows red at about 500°C, is cherry red at about 700°C, is yellow at 1000°C, and becomes white hot at 1200°C. These changes in color have been utilized in devices called optical pyrometers. In its simplest form the optical pyrometer consists of a telescope that has a red glass filter mounted

Figure 2–10. The first optical pyrometer.

in it and a small electric lamp bulb as shown in Figure 2–11. When the pyrometer is directed toward an object hot enough to glow, an observer looking through the telescope sees the dark lamp filament against the bright background of the object. The lamp filament is connected in series with a battery and a variable resistor, permitting its brightness to be adjusted until the brightness of the filament just matches the brightness of the background. From previous calibration of the instrument, the current through the lamp may be related to the temperature of the object observed.

There are also pyrometers used in relatively low temperature work that are sensitive to infrared radiation only. In the temperature range from 10° to 1000°C most of the radiation emitted by a hot body is in the infrared region. Several commercially available infrared thermometers make use of thermistors or groups of thermocouples onto which the radiation is directed.

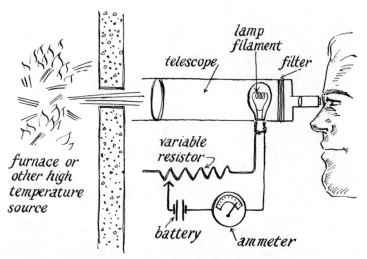

Figure 2–11. The elements of an optical pyrometer.

Another type of infrared thermometer utilizes what is known as a thermal imaging technique. Here infrared radiation forms a heat image of the field of view in a camera-like device. Figure 2–12 shows an image produced by such a device. In one such device called an Evaporagraph the image formed by the infrared radiation on a thin nitrocellulose membrane alters the thickness of an oil film condensed on the back of the membrane. This variation in thickness causes a beam of white light that is directed onto the oil film to be reflected as different colors, thus giving rise to a colored image. This colored image is formed as a result of the same phenomenon that produces the brilliant colors frequently seen when light is reflected from a soap bubble or from a thin layer of oil floating on water; the colors are formed by interference effects between trains of light waves reflected at opposite surfaces of a thin film. The interference colors may be used to

Figure 2-12. An image produced by means of thermography. In this scheme the hotter the area being scanned by the thermal imaging camera, the whiter the image it produces on the film. On this thermograph the pipe bowl is very hot and hence very white while the tip of the nose and the edge of the ear appear relatively cold and hence dark. This may be due to the contraction of the blood vessels that occurs during smoking.

determine the temperature of an object being surveyed to about $\pm 2°C$. The temperature determination depends on the fact that the rate of evaporation or condensation of the oil on the membrane varies with the radiant energy received from the viewed object.

In the next chapter we consider the relation between heat and other forms of energy as expressed in the law of conservation of energy. As we shall see, temperature measurements played an important role in establishing this law and still play an important role in applying the law to a great variety of problems.

chapter three
bookkeeper's delight

"Practical" men have long dreamed of getting something for nothing. Some of these men are recorded in history as the Robber Barons of the nineteenth century, and may be regarded as having achieved their dreams. We, however, are here concerned with the failures—the men who tried to invent "something for nothing" machines.

Let us imagine a miller, possibly a descendant of the one Chaucer wrote about. Our miller, being a clever chap, recognized many advantages in owning a mill that could be set up far from a flowing stream. Further, being industrious as well as practical, he set about inventing a mill that required no stream. He envisaged a great tank of water above a waterwheel. Water would flow from a hole in the bottom of the tank and cause the wheel to turn. The turning wheel would grind the grain and operate a pump to return the water to the tank, as illustrated in Figure 3–1. Unfortunately, the pump could never return enough water to the tank to keep the mill operating.

The miller tried to invent a useful perpetual motion machine—what today we call a perpetual motion machine of the first kind. All such mechanical perpetual motion machines are intended to accomplish some sort of work and to restore themselves to their original condition so they can continue doing work *ad infinitum*, all without the aid of a flowing stream or other source of energy.

Possibly the most common approach to intended mechanical perpetual motion machines has been by way of the overbalanced wheel, often inspired by a misunderstanding of the purpose of a flywheel. A common form of the overbalanced wheel is shown in Figure 3–2. This particular wheel is intended to move forever in a clockwise direction because the greater leverage exerted by the

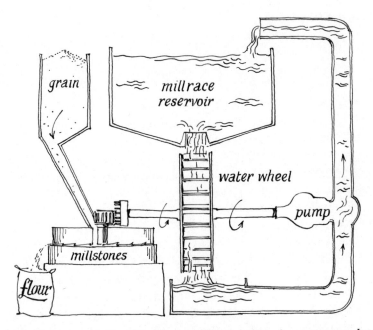

Figure 3–1. The miller's mill without a millstream. His scheme supposes that part of the energy from the water that leaves the tank is used to mill the grain and part is used to pump all of the water back into the tank. This type of device is called a perpetual motion machine of the first kind because it violates the first law of thermodynamics.

weights on the descending side will overbalance the lesser leverage of the ascending weights. This is a roundabout way of saying that the falling weights will do more work along the descending path than is required to raise them along the ascending path. But today even beginning students of mechanics know that the work one can get out of the falling weights in such an arrangement is independent of their distance from the center of the wheel. Stated more formally: Since the changes in potential energy of the ascending and descending weights are exactly the same, there can be nothing left over to run the wheel.

Nowadays rational men refuse to invest in mechanical perpetual motion machines because such machines would have to operate in violation of the law of conservation of energy, which is rightly regarded as being as certain as death and taxes. Evidence that natural philosophers, as contrasted to "practical" men, have long recognized the impossibility of perpetual motion is provided by the decision of the Paris Academy of Sciences in 1775 to consider no more claims for such machines.

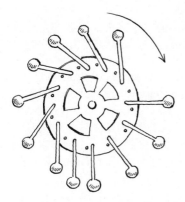

Figure 3–2
Illustration of the overbalanced wheel that has been used in many machines designed to work forever without the aid of any outside agency.

Pioneering work by Archimedes, Galileo, Huygens, Newton, Leibniz, d'Alembert, Lagrange, Young, and others (in areas now labeled Greece, Italy, Holland, England, Germany, and France) on falling weights, centrifugal force, and the general laws of motion of material bodies provided the basis for the law of conservation of energy as applied to mechanical systems. The accounts by some of the early investigators read today more like theology than science, as illustrated by the following excerpt from Descartes's *Principles of Philosophy:*

> . . . it seems to me evident that it is nothing other than God, Who by His Almighty power created matter with motion and rest in its parts, and Who thereafter conserves in the

universe by His ordinary operations as much of motion and
of rest as He put in it in the first creation.

The idea that heat and motion are intimately connected was
familiar to the Greeks. Democritus, Heraclitus, and Plato all recognized that heat and cold were relevant to the workings of nature
and saw a connection between heat and motion. Plato was fairly
explicit when he said "For heat and fire which generate and sustain other things, are themselves begotten by impact and friction:
but this is motion. Are not these the origin of fire?"

Francis Bacon's *Novum Organum* (1620) is often acknowledged as containing the first scientifically based statement that
heat is a form of motion. Bacon has a well-deserved reputation for
contributing to the present view that observation and experimentation are essential parts of our efforts to understand the workings
of nature. Further, his view that an important function of science
was "the endowment of human life with new inventions and
riches" was taken up and applied fruitfully by the founders of the
Royal Society in England. Although it is true that Bacon anticipated the important discovery of a connection between motion
and heat, it is a gross exaggeration to say that he is the father of
the scientific method or even that he saw this particular connection as the result of sensible scientific application of his inductive
method.

Bacon carried out his "studies" of heat as an intended object
lesson on the proper methods for scientific investigation. He believed that original research could be systematized into the making of lists of facts derived from observation, which was to be
followed by Aristotelian thought that would lead infallibly to the
desired understanding. Brief consideration of the "facts" that
Bacon listed should dispel forever the notion that he conducted a
scientific investigation. For instance, he categorized pepper, mus-
tard, and wool clothing as hot and said that moonbeams are cold,
although they resemble hot sunbeams. Without proceeding

further into the details of Bacon's work, we conclude along with several natural philosophers of the seventeenth century and later that the methods of Galileo and d'Alembert, rather than Bacon, are the essence of fruitful scientific investigation.

In the years between 1660 and 1675 Robert Boyle reported the results of his experiments concerning heat. He was the first to express a connection between motion and heat in almost the same terms we use today. For instance, he specifically declared heat to be a motion of the tiny parts (what we call atoms and molecules) of matter. In view of the importance attached more than a century later to Count Rumford's concern with the heat developed in boring cannons, it is interesting to note that Boyle also recognized and cited this heat development as support for his views. Boyle correctly recognized that heat generated or imparted to a body by mechanical means is "new" heat; he was thus getting close to formulating what we now call the first law of thermodynamics. Although Boyle's contributions to the early study of heat were important, it is not to be thought that he contributed no confusion. For instance, he often wrote of "atoms of fire" and mistakenly attributed the gain in weight of oxidized metals to the capture of such "atoms."

Leibniz' recipe for the study of mechanics included more mathematics and less theology than did the work of Descartes. He was the first to state in reasonably explicit terms that energy is conserved. His *vis viva* and *vis mortua* were just twice our modern kinetic energy and potential energy. Leibniz recognized that one could be converted to the other, but that the sum was conserved in mechanical processes. Jean d'Alembert, an illegitimate child who was left on the steps of a church but who otherwise separated science and theology, wrote:

> . . . I have turned my thoughts away from causes of motion to consider solely the motions that they produce; and that I have entirely excluded forces inherent in bodies in motion,

obscure and metaphysical entities which can only cast shadows on a science that is in itself clear.

Thus d'Alembert might be considered a principal founder of the "operational method" that has been applied so usefully to a variety of problems by Poincaré, Bridgman, and others.

Leibniz also recognized a connection between motion and heat. When he was asked what becomes of the *vis viva* (kinetic energy) of two inelastic spheres when they collide and thereby come to rest, he wrote in reply:

> It is true that the wholes lose it in reference to their total movement; but it is received by the particles; they being agitated inwardly by the force of the collision. Thus the loss ensues only in appearance. The forces are not destroyed, but dissipated among the minute parts.

If Leibniz had been equipped with sensitive thermometers, he might have discovered experimentally that the spheres in question actually become hotter when a collision converts the *vis viva* of the entire spheres into molecular agitation of their constituent atoms.

Since most of the ideas of Boyle, Leibniz, and others of their times who favored a motion theory of heat were soundly based and could account for the observable facts of the day, we might wonder why the caloric theory to be discussed shortly was generally more popular for many years. First of all, we should recognize that Boyle and the others who developed the motion theory attributed heat to motion of the minute particles (atoms) of matter. Thus the production of heat from motion of a cannon borer could be explained as the conversion of one kind of motion to another. Similar explanations accounted for other observations. But quantitative calculations were at that stage generally impossible. Even more important, the invisible motions of the atoms were reasonably regarded at that time as speculation that could not be confirmed in any independent way.

Although people today who know little of anything scientific scoff at the caloric theory, this theory was supported by most of the best minds in Europe before the end of the eighteenth century and was not finally laid to rest until the middle of the nineteenth century. As an illustration of the respectability of the caloric theory, we note that the Académie des Sciences in 1738 offered prizes for the best essays on heat and selected Voltaire, Euler, and the Marquis du Châtelet as winners, all of whom supported ideas basic to the caloric theory of heat phenomena. This caloric theory could account very well for most of the observations having to do with heat and for many years had it all over the motion theory in terms of numerical calculations in agreement with experimental results.

The name "caloric" for the "imponderable matter of heat" had been originated in 1789 by Lavoisier, but the theory itself was considerably older. In 1808 John Dalton concisely summarized the generally accepted notion of heat as follows: "The most probable opinion concerning the nature of caloric, is, that of its being an elastic fluid of great subtility, the particles of which repel one another, but are attracted by all other bodies."

Various chemical reactions, friction, and the vigorous compression of a gas all *apparently* produce heat. But what is actually *observed* is an increase in temperature, so the adherents of the caloric theory regarded the production of heat in these processes as an unjustified assumption and chose instead to explain the observed temperature increases in terms of heat or caloric already existing. The rise of temperature on compression of a gas was explained as due to a release of latent heat that was made necessary by the decrease in volume of the gas (recall that the particles of caloric were supposed to repel each other). The temperature rises produced by friction were also believed to be due to a sort of squeezing out of latent caloric. The calorists were similarly able to account for a variety of other phenomena. Most striking of all, the caloric theory could be applied to numerical calculation of relations involving such quantities as specific heats and velocities of sound in gases. A variety of experiments confirmed these calculations.

As Mott-Smith has written about the caloric theory: "After someone else has killed the enemy, it is easy enough to kick the corpse. But it was a different matter to tackle him when he was alive and vigorous." Caloric theory corpse-kicking may have reached its height between about 1860 and 1880 among British physicists, who at the time had no qualms about accepting the currently popular theory of the mysterious fluid called *aether*. Lord Rayleigh's nationalistic view that a large proportion of outstanding English scientists always favored the idea that heat is motion rather than the caloric theory is unsupported by the contemporary statements of most of the scientists concerned.

During the active life of the caloric theory, it succeeded very well in accounting for the behavior of heat once it was produced, but suffered considerably in efforts to account for the heat produced by friction. Most of these difficulties centered on the conclusion of Count Rumford that heat could be produced without limit by friction. As a result of his experiments on the heating effects associated with boring of cannons, Rumford stated in a report to the Royal Society:

> In reasoning on this subject, we must not forget that most remarkable circumstance, that the source of heat generated by friction in these experiments appeared evidently to be inexhaustible. It is hardly necessary to add that anything which any insulated body or system of bodies can continue to furnish without limitation cannot possibly be a material substance; and it appears to me to be extremely difficult, if not quite impossible, to form any distinct idea of anything capa-

ble of being excited and communicated in these experiments, except it be motion.[1]

Without taking too much advantage of the benefits of hindsight, it does seem reasonable to express some surprise that the experiments and clear reasoning of Rumford did not immediately squelch the caloric theory and its picture of heat as a fluid substance. The persisting faith in the caloric theory is especially remarkable when we note that Humphry Davy, who apparently retained his faith in most of the caloric theory, also did ingenious experiments on the development of heat by friction. He caused two blocks of ice to be rubbed together by a clockwork mechanism, and succeeded in converting almost all the ice to water, even though the whole apparatus was kept at the freezing point. Perhaps James Conant provided the explanation for the long life of the caloric theory after it was no longer tenable on purely experimental grounds when he wrote: "We can put it down as one of the principles learned from the history of science that a theory is only overthrown by a better theory, never merely by contradictory facts."

Before proceeding with accounts of the experiments and especially the theory that finally displaced the caloric theory, a few more words about Count Rumford may prove interesting. Although he was frequently much occupied with nonscientific pursuits, his abiding interest in the subject of this book is made clear by the following words he wrote at age fifty-one: "To engage in experiments on Heat was always one of my most agreeable occu-

---

[1] *Teachers of thermodynamics frequently describe Rumford's cannon-boring experiment in which he employed a team of horses to turn the drill bit in the cannon muzzle. Those who pose the question "Now what quantity is produced without limit in this experiment?" always receive the shouted answer "Horse manure."*

pations. . . . I was often prevented by other matters from devoting my attention to it, but whenever I could snatch a moment I returned to it anew, and always with increased interest."

Recognition and experimental verification of the equivalence of heat and work as different forms of energy took place in convincing fashion between 1840 and 1850. But in the intervening years after Rumford's cannon-boring in Munich near the turn of the century, a number of men were on the verge of recognizing and verifying this grand conception of conservation of energy that we call the first law of thermodynamics. Among these almost-discoverers were William Grove (an English physician), Marc Seguin (a French railway engineer), Karl Mohr (a German chemist), Sadi Carnot (a French engineer), Justus von Liebig (a German chemist), and Michael Faraday (a nearly universal scientist). All of these men had some glimmer of an idea of a conservation law, but none was sufficiently precise in his formulations to develop anything either convincing or useful.

Most of the credit for discovery and confirmation of the first law as a generalization of the conservation of energy goes to Hermann von Helmholtz (a German physician, largely devoted to physiology), James Prescott Joule (son of a prosperous English brewer, he was tutored informally by John Dalton and others), and Julius Mayer (a German physician). Current nonscientific attitudes toward these men and their works are sometimes amusing. For instance, nonphysicists may smile (physicists rarely smile while being condescending to nonphysicists) when they read in otherwise excellent books by physicists that it is surprising that none of these admirable founders of the first law of thermodynamics was a physicist. Some chemists take another approach, claiming Joule as one of them on the flimsy basis of his having been tutored as a child for a couple of years by chemist John Dalton. Although these parochial attitudes are little more than a trivial joke today, they had an important bearing on the acceptance of the early work, especially that of Mayer. Nationalism also contributed to the lack of recognition of Mayer.

Our story of the last steps in the discovery and confirmation of the first law begins with Julius Robert Mayer. In 1840 this twenty-seven-year-old physician sailed to Java as ship's doctor. While bleeding patients in the tropics, he observed that their blood was a much brighter red than that taken from veins of patients in Germany. Since it was known that the red color of venous blood was due to oxygen that had not been used for oxidation of body fuel, Mayer had no trouble in deducing that venous blood in Java was redder than venous blood in Germany because less combustion is required to supply the needed body heat in Java than in Germany. Some sixty years earlier Crawford, Lavoisier, and Laplace had all reached this same conclusion that less internal combustion is required when the body is in warm surroundings than when it is in cold surroundings.

At this point Mayer took one more step, one that had proved too difficult for all the others who had already recognized part of the significance of differences in redness of venous blood. Mayer concluded that the heat developed by internal combustion should be balanced against the body's heat loss to the surroundings *and* the work the body performs. That is, Mayer was thinking and soon saying (in archaic language) that heat and work are equivalent, being merely two different manifestations of a general property called *energy*.

Although he regarded the logic of his statement as very convincing, Mayer recognized that some direct experimental verification was needed. But he had no facilities for doing the necessary experiments, nor money to buy equipment. Further, much of his time was occupied by the medical practice he had taken up in Germany on his return from Java. The few experiments he was able to undertake did point in the right direction, but were inconclusive because of poor experimental techniques or at least poor reporting. For instance, Mayer found that he could cause water to increase in temperature merely by shaking it. But his account of this experiment did not make it clear how he could be sure that the increase in temperature was not due to transfer of heat from his hands to the water.

Mayer then showed a true measure of his greatness by doing the best he could with the results of other people's experiments. First, he resurrected a forgotten experiment carried out in France by Gay-Lussac in 1807. Gay-Lussac had placed two chambers in an insulated box and connected them by means of a tube containing a stopcock, as indicated in Figure 3–3. Thermometers were in-

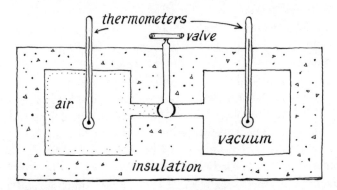

Figure 3–3. Illustration of the forgotten experiment by Gay-Lussac in 1807 that provided evidence in support of Mayer's ideas.

serted in each chamber. One chamber contained air, while the other was evacuated. When the stopcock was opened, air rushed into the previously evacuated chamber. Although the caloric theory was specific in predicting that the temperature ought to drop, Gay-Lussac observed that final readings of the thermometers were the same as the initial readings.

Mayer's explanation of this experiment, which had baffled other scientists until they conveniently forgot all about it, was clear and simple. In the usual expansion of a gas against a piston the gas must do work in pushing the piston. The temperature of the gas falls because some of its internal energy is converted into external work. But in Gay-Lussac's experiment the gas had expanded into a vacuum so that it did no work on the surroundings and consequently lost no energy to cause a drop in temperature.

Mayer took still one more important step. Even in his day, it had long been known that the specific heat [2] of a gas depends on how that specific heat is measured. The two most common specific heats are those determined under constant pressure conditions and under constant volume conditions, with constant pressure specific heats being greater than constant volume specific heats. Mayer reasoned that the extra heat required in the constant pressure process (in which the volume increases as temperature increases) was consumed in doing work of expansion against the constant pressure imposed by the surroundings. By using already known values of the constant pressure and constant volume specific heats of air, Mayer was able to calculate the numerical relation between units of mechanical work and of heat. In the language we use today, he calculated the mechanical equivalent of heat.

Mayer submitted the first written account of his discovery to Poggendorff's *Annalen der Physik*, but was refused publication. A revised account of his work was accepted by Liebig and published in *Annalen der Chemie und Pharmacie* in 1842. Then in 1845 he wrote and had privately printed a pamphlet titled "Or-

[2] *The specific heat of a substance is defined as the quantity of heat, usually expressed in calories, required to cause an increase of 1°C in the temperature of 1 gram of the substance. The calorie for many years was defined as the quantity of heat required to raise the temperature of 1 gram of water (under standard conditions), 1°C. It is now defined almost identically in terms of the joule, a quantity of electrical energy that provides a better standard. See Appendix A.*

ganic Motion in Its Connection with Nutrition." Two more privately printed accounts of his work were published in 1848 and 1851. By 1851 Mayer had learned of Joule's work in England and acknowledged him as an independent discoverer, but claimed priority for himself.

There was little of the reasonable opposition that Mayer probably expected before his ideas were accepted. Most of the scientific world ignored him. His neighbors, the local press, and those few scientists who troubled to read about his work ridiculed and abused him. Worst of all, Mayer saw others duplicate many of his discoveries, reach the same conclusions, and be honored for *their* important contributions to science. It was only when Mayer was an old man that the efforts of Clausius and Helmholtz in Germany and Tyndall in England resulted in some of the recognition Mayer deserved.

Although James Joule and Julius Mayer often pursued scientifically parallel paths, their lives and studies of heat were largely different. In 1837 at age nineteen Joule built an electric engine operated by a battery, apparently with a view toward the future conversion of his father's brewery from steam to electric power. But Joule was more than a rich-boy hobbyist playing with machines. He began to make measurements of the output of his engine (work accomplished) and the electrical input. Output measurements were made reasonably simple in terms of weights lifted by the engine, but electrical measurements at that time were in such a state that he had to design and then build his own instruments for his input measurements.

In the course of his work with electric engines, Joule measured the heat developed by passage of electric current. He found that the rate of heat production was proportional to the square of the current times the resistance of the wire carrying the current. Joule's paper reporting this important result (now called Joule's law) was at first refused publication by the Royal Society but was later published after it had been reduced to the grand total of twenty lines.

These early (1837–1840) investigations showed Joule that a battery-driven electric engine could not hope to compete with steam power, so he turned his attention to the mechanical generation of electricity by means of the primitive dynamo invented by Faraday.[3] In this simple machine a current was produced by revolving a spool of wire between the poles of a magnet. Joule found that the current so generated caused heat to be developed in the wires of the spool and again confirmed his "heat equals current squared times resistance" equation. He reasoned that the source of this heat was the work that went into turning the handle that revolved the spool of wire. Then he set about confirming his reasoning by measuring the work put into turning the handle. His first results were inaccurate, but gave him the confidence to continue.

Joule soon realized that the conversion of work to heat could be simplified by leaving out the connecting electrical link. He made measurements of the heat produced when water is forced to flow through small holes in a piston and also made measurements of heat effects associated with compression and expansion of gases. In 1843 his description of these experiments at a scientific meeting in Cork attracted no attention. Despite this discouragement, Joule continued his measurements.

Joule recognized that more accurate experiments were needed and finally settled upon the apparatus pictured schematically in Figure 3–4 as being most suitable for his purposes. An insulated

---

[3] *We paraphrase a conversation reported to have taken place in Faraday's laboratory shortly after he had made his discoveries leading to the electric dynamo.*

Eminent British Politician: "What good is it?"

Faraday: "I don't know yet, but someday you'll tax it."

vessel containing water was stirred by a set of revolving vanes intermeshing with a set of fixed vanes. The revolving vanes were operated by a system of descending weights so that the work input could be precisely known. Since the temperature rises were generally less than one degree, it was necessary that Joule use very

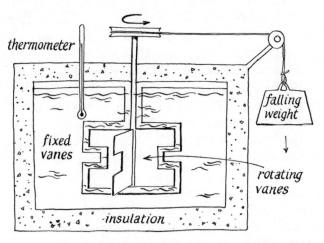

Figure 3–4. A schematic of Joule's apparatus for measuring the mechanical equivalent of heat. The weight is allowed to fall, causing it to do work on the water by means of the paddle. The stirring of the water causes its temperature to rise. Since the heat required to raise the temperature of a given quantity of water was already known (from its specific heat), a numerical connection between heat and work in terms of a common effect was established.

sensitive thermometers. He had the needed thermometers made specially for him, and then he tested and standardized them. The result was that Joule's temperature measurements were the most accurate that had been made up to that time. In the end, he equated the work done by the falling weights to the amount of heat that would be required to produce the same effect in the water.

Joule's best value for the mechanical equivalent of heat was 772.5 foot-pounds (ft-lb) equal to one British thermal unit (Btu) of heat. The accepted value today is 778.16, which differs by less than 1 per cent from Joule's value. Considering the facilities Joule had to work with, we must conclude that he was an exceptionally able experimentalist.

In the years between 1845 and 1850 Joule gave several talks on his results and published detailed accounts in British scientific journals. Most British scientists were reluctant to accept Joule's two conclusions: (1) Heat and work are equivalent, being different forms or manifestations of energy, and (2) the numerical factor governing conversion of work to heat (each expressed in common units such as foot-pounds or calories) was accurately known from his water-stirring experiments and approximately known from calculations like those made by Mayer. The essence of the general argument against Joule was that he had only fractions of a degree to prove his points.

During this period from 1845 to 1850 when Joule was improving both his measurements and his calculations, his work attracted the attention of William Thomson, later Lord Kelvin. Although Thomson was only twenty-six years of age in 1850, he had already made important scientific discoveries, including the first steps toward establishment of a truly absolute temperature scale that was independent of the properties of any particular substance (mercury, alcohol, air, etc.) used as a thermometric fluid. Although Thomson recognized that there was merit in the work of Joule, he remained an adherent of the caloric theory, presumably because of his great admiration for the earlier work of Carnot. It was only about 1852, largely as a result of the work of Helmholtz and Clausius, that Thomson came to reject the old caloric theory and to accept the idea of Mayer and Joule that conservation of energy applies to both heat and work.

In 1847 at the age of twenty-six Hermann von Helmholtz wrote a paper in which he set out and justified the general law of conservation of energy in more convincing and general terms than had either Mayer or Joule. Poggendorff's *Annalen der Physik* maintained consistency with its earlier rejection of Mayer's paper by also rejecting this work of Helmholtz. So Helmholtz presented his ideas at a Physical Society meeting in Berlin and had the paper published privately.

Nowadays we deny the possibility of perpetual motion machines because such machines would have to operate contrary to the law of conservation of energy. Helmholtz reversed this procedure by taking the impossibility of perpetual motion machines as his fundamental axiom. He could not *prove* this axiom, but he did point out that no one had ever built a perpetual motion machine, and also emphasized that Carnot and Clapeyron had earlier proceeded from a similar denial to important and well-verified laws concerning heat. Helmholtz then showed that this denial of perpetual motion machines required that energy be conserved. He further showed that heat (small-scale motion) and work (large-scale motion) must both be considered as energy and that it is the total that is conserved, rather than either heat or work separately. Helmholtz then proceeded in clear, scientific language to show that the experiments of Joule were in general agreement with the results of calculations like those carried out by Mayer.

Helmholtz went further than either Mayer or Joule in applying the generalized law of conservation of energy. He used the requirement that energy accounts (including both heat and work) must balance as a tool in solving a variety of problems, which we illustrate with one important example. Helmholtz showed that the electrical discharge of a Leyden jar should oscillate and die out in a certain manner. He reasoned that the potential energy of the charges on the undischarged jar is converted into the kinetic energy of the electrical discharge current. But this electric current that dissipates the excess negative charge on one wall of the Leyden jar overshoots the mark (much as the swing of a pendulum overshoots the "neutral" state of being at rest at the mid-point of its arc) and causes the other wall of the Leyden jar to have an excess of electrons. This overshooting is followed by another discharge in the form of a smaller electric current flowing in the direction opposite to that of the first discharge current. This second discharge current again overshoots the mark of neutrality on the jar and is followed by a still smaller third discharge current, this time in the direction of the first discharge. Gradually these oscillating discharges die out as their energy is converted to heat in the electric circuit consisting of the Leyden jar and external wires.

Following the general explanation by Helmholtz, William Thomson worked out a detailed mathematical description of the oscillations. A few years later Fedderson observed the oscillations experimentally and provided general confirmation of Thomson's equations. After still a few more years, Hertz applied this oscillation to the production of the electric waves that now form the basis of radio communications.

The ideas and methods of Mayer, Joule, and Helmholtz gradually won acceptance, initially because of the fine experimental work of Joule and the logical development and expression by Helmholtz. Then in 1850 the German physicist Rudolf Clausius entered the picture. He succeeded in combining the work of Mayer, Joule, and Helmholtz on conservation of energy with the earlier work of Carnot and Clapeyron on entropy in both useful and convincing fashion. He also originated the terminology used today: The first law of thermodynamics is the great generalization of energy conservation and the second law of thermodynamics is the entropy principle concerned with the degradation of energy.

We now turn briefly to careful and, we hope, clear statements of the first law of thermodynamics. These statements are less difficult than the fancy name implies.

The first law is stated concisely as follows: *Energy may be changed from one form to another but is neither created nor destroyed.* In order to go from this verbal statement to mathematical statements appropriate to making deductions or merely doing energy accounting, it is necessary to list the relevant forms of energy and then to express in an equation the constancy of total energy in terms of these various forms of energy.

We begin by dividing energy into heat and work. Work can then be subdivided into mechanical work, electrical work, gravitational work, etc. The next step is to state what we mean by the word *system*. By *system* we mean any particular part of the universe. A thermodynamic system might be the gas confined in a cylinder closed at one end with a piston, or it might be an entire plant for generation of electrical power. Similarly, a thermodynamic system might be a Thermos jug containing a few chemicals dissolved in water, or it might be a large and complicated apparatus devoted to conversion of gaseous ethylene from a petroleum refinery into polyethylene bags.

Now let us suppose that some thermodynamic system undergoes a process in which it is changed in several ways but in the end returns to its original state or condition. The first law tells us that the total energy of the system must be conserved, meaning that the energy of the system is the same at the end of the cyclical process as it was at the beginning. This conservation of energy can be expressed as

$$E_2 = E_1 \text{ or } E_2 - E_1 = 0$$

where E_1 and E_2 represent energies at the beginning and end of the process. We can also write $\Delta E = 0$ where ΔE is shorthand for $E_2 - E_1$.

From the italicized statement of the first law given earlier we may say that the energy change undergone by a system is equal to the energy gained in the form of heat minus the energy lost as a result of work done on the surroundings. This statement is expressed concisely by

$$E_2 - E_1 = Q - W$$

where Q is the heat absorbed by the system and W is the work done on the surroundings by the system.

Because Q represents heat absorbed by the system, $+Q$ means heat absorbed and $-Q$ means heat evolved or lost by the system. If we have a flame under a boiler or other body being heated, Q is negative for the flame system which is losing heat to its surroundings and Q is positive for the boiler system which is absorbing heat from its surroundings.

Because W represents work done by the system on the surroundings, $+W$ means that the system accomplishes work on its surroundings while $-W$ means that work is done on the system by the surroundings.

The first law, as summarized by $\Delta E = 0$ for cyclical processes and $\Delta E = Q - W$ for all processes, gives us a sound basis for useful application of accounting procedures to phenomena involving heat and work. In the following paragraph we give a simple illustration of this aspect of the first law, which might well be called "Bookkeeper's Delight" because the accounts always balance.

Suppose that a system absorbs 120 calories from one part of its surroundings and does 150 calories of work on another part of its surroundings. What is ΔE for the system? Since heat absorbed corresponds to positive Q and work done on the surroundings also corresponds to positive W, we have

$$\Delta E = Q - W = (+120) - (+150) = -30 \text{ calories}$$

Remembering that ΔE is shorthand for $E_{\text{final}} - E_{\text{initial}}$ or $E_2 - E_1$, we also have $E_2 - E_1 = -30$ calories. The energy of our system has diminished by 30 calories and has lost some of its capability for doing work. This decreased capability for doing work might appear in the form of a lower temperature for the system.

Before proceeding in the next chapter to applications of the first law, it is interesting to consider a little "it might have been" history.

In the years between 1800 and 1840 a number of men were close
to recognizing or establishing the first law. One of these was Sadi
Carnot, who is justly famed as the discoverer in 1824 of what
we now call the second law. At the time of his great discovery
Carnot (like most other scientists at that time) believed in the
existence of a caloric fluid. But in unpublished notes written between 1824 and his death at age thirty-six in 1832, Carnot indicated growing skepticism about the caloric theory. Further, he
described experiments that ought to be done to settle the matter.
A partial list of experiments he suggested is given as follows in
approximately Carnot's own words: (1) To repeat Rumford's
experiments on the drilling of a metal, but to measure the motive
power consumed at the same time as the heat produced. (2) To
agitate water vigorously. (3) To strike a piece of lead, to measure
the motive power consumed and the heat produced. (4) Improve
experiments with Gay-Lussac's two equal vessels, one empty and
the other filled with air.

It is quite clear that Carnot anticipated some of the ideas of
Mayer and Joule. Had he lived a few years longer, could Carnot
have seen the first law with the vision of Mayer, done precise
measurements with the great skill of Joule, and provided both
logical development and clear exposition in the manner of Helmholtz? Possibly. If so, Carnot would have been the Father of both
the first and second laws.

Although all of the men mentioned in this chapter as partial
founders of the first law were often ignored by their scientific
colleagues and sometimes subjected to ridicule, it is pleasant to
think that each of these harassed individuals could occasionally
comfort himself with the idea, if not the words, of Thoreau's statement that "Any man more right than his neighbors constitutes a
majority of one."

chapter four
energy: capital, income, and expense

The idea that energy is conserved is not one that is difficult to grasp. In fact, once heat and work were clearly defined and the notion of caloric was discarded, the law of conservation of energy seemed to follow rather naturally. It is an idea, one can argue, that has universal appeal. Henry Bent, an American chemist, described the broad-based appeal of the first law in the following way:

> Mathematicians [believe the first law is true] because they believe it is a fact of observation; observers because they believe it is a theorem of mathematics; philosophers because they believe it is aesthetically satisfying, or because they believe new forms of energy can always be invented to make it true. A few neither believe nor disbelieve it; these people maintain that the First Law is a procedure for bookkeeping energy changes, and about bookkeeping procedures it should be asked, not are they true or false, but are they useful.

In this chapter we examine man's energy accounts—his expenditures, his income, his capital reserves—and use the first law to balance the energy accounts.

The Industrial Revolution began some 4000 years after man learned to fabricate reasonably complex objects out of metal. Why the big delay when the tools for this revolution were already at hand or could be made? One reason was that the philosophers and teachers of Greece and Rome considered technology unworthy of their attention. One result of this attitude was that craftsmen of considerable ingenuity built complex devices that were used only to accomplish trivial tasks. For example, Hero of

Alexandria in the first century A.D. constructed a small steam turbine (see Figure 4–1) that was used primarily as a toy.

Let us now consider some of the changes that finally brought this attitude toward technology to an end. Technological innovation or widespread industrialization was accelerated by the convergence of two forces: (1) the acceptance of the idea that human slavery was morally wrong—that labor must be paid for, and (2) the slow but steady growth of available *surplus energy*.

sphere with water/steam

Figure 4–1. Hero's aeolipile was developed as a toy but illustrated the principle of the steam turbine which plays a central role in the generation of electricity today. The aeolipile consists of a hollow sphere mounted on trunions and partly filled with water. When the water boils, the steam escapes from the tangential outlets and the resulting reaction forces cause the sphere to turn in its trunions.

The first of these forces is part of the history of the breakdown of feudalistic agrarian societies, the development of constitutional governments, and the slow spreading of libertarian ideas throughout Europe as it crept out of the Dark Ages.

The other force, *surplus energy*, has been fully recognized by only a few social scientists, such as Fred Cottrell, who have studied the development of our industrial society. By surplus energy we mean the energy available to man in excess of the energy he has invested in obtaining his available energy. We may illustrate the idea of surplus energy by considering a farmer in a primitive society or even in a frontier society of a few generations ago. The farmer plants his seeds, cares for and finally harvests his crops, all with expenditure of energy. If his harvest has been sufficiently bountiful, he has seeds for next year, food for his family and work animals, and still has some food left over. This extra produce is surplus energy, which he can spend in a variety of ways. First, he may sell or barter his surplus food for things that will make his life more pleasant. Or he may use his surplus to obtain more work animals and thereby increase the size or productivity of his farm and raise even more surplus energy next year. Or he might, in effect, use his surplus food to buy free time for himself, which he may then devote to construction or even invention of a machine that will eventually lead to production of still more surplus energy.

This idea may be applied equally well to industrial workers. For example, the first English coal miners were able in a day to mine coal with a heating value about 500 times larger than the heating value of the food the miner consumed that day. If that coal were burned in a steam engine of only 1 per cent efficiency, it would yield about 50 times as much mechanical energy as the miner expended in getting the coal from the ground. Thus the miner created 49 man-days of surplus energy by his day in the mine. That energy, in many cases, created additional surplus energy, and so on. As can be seen by these simple examples, this process is self-catalyzing and has not yet stopped. Technological innovation begets more technological innovation.

Does the availability of surplus energy today automatically assure a society of a high standard of living? Figure 4–2, a plot of data gathered by the United Nations, shows an exponential relation between energy consumption and average yearly per capita

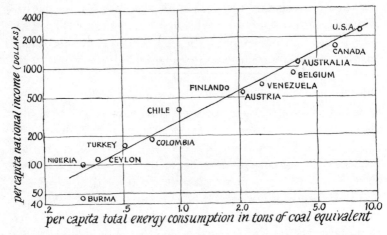

Figure 4-2. The exponential relation between average yearly per capita income and energy consumption in 1958 as shown on a logarithmic plot. (After Hartley in *United Nations Publication Sales* No. 63.1.2.)

income. In general, it can be concluded that industrialization, economic growth, and material well-being are almost always associated with a rising and high level of energy consumption.

Although it appears to be certain that availability of considerable surplus energy is necessary to a high material standard of living, it is simply not enough to ensure that a society will be prosperous. Other resources, including political, social, cultural, and environmental factors, can play roles as important as the availability of energy. For example, in 1956 Saudi Arabia had a per capita income of approximately $80 per year but it produced from its petroleum reserves energy equivalent to 10 metric tons of coal per capita. Switzerland, in the same year, had an equivalent energy production per capita of only 1.75 metric tons of coal and a per capita income of approximately $1200. At the same time energy consumption in Switzerland was about 3.2 metric tons equivalent, almost twice its own production and nearly 17 times the per capita energy *use* in Saudi Arabia. Switzerland was able to make up its energy deficit simply by importing what was required. It is extremely difficult to import the political, social, and cultural factors that combine with energy availability and use to determine a country's progress toward a higher standard of living.

As industrialization proceeded, man needed a way to measure the rate at which energy was being expended in a process. The unit decided upon by James Watt, a great English inventor, was the *horsepower*. Some people think that Watt chose this unit so that he could compare for advertising purposes the steam engines he was building and selling with the size of the team of horses required to do the same job.[1]

Watt found that a "representative" horse could do work at a rate of 33,000 foot-pounds per minute. That is, an average horse could raise a weight of 33,000 pounds a height of 1 foot in 1 minute, or raise 330 pounds a height of 100 feet in 1 minute, or any product of weight times distance that equals 33,000 foot-pounds, as shown in Figure 4-3.

Prior to industrialization, the prime mover generally used for heavy labor was the ox, but for jobs that required faster movement the horse was better. It has been found that camels deliver energy at twice the rate horses do, but require considerably more space for movement. In addition, when considering animate power, time must be allowed for resting and eating. The following table compares various power sources.

Some people have estimated man's *continuous* duty rated output at about $\frac{1}{30}$ horsepower; this number allows time for rest, eating,

[1] *Had Watt been more scientist and less salesman, he might have chosen a laboratory animal such as the guinea pig for his standard. Then advertisements for today's autos might have been able to go to superlatives with statements like: "1,272,000 pigpower to keep you cruising at turnpike speeds all day (without even a hint of odor)."*

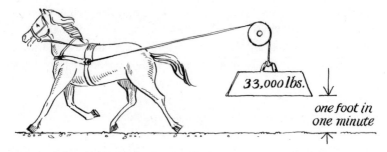

33,000 lbs.

*one foot in
one minute*

Figure 4–3. A horsepower is defined as a rate of work equivalent to raising 33,000 pounds 1 foot in 1 minute.

Power Available from Various Sources

energy source	force (Push or Pull) exerted (in Pounds)	rate of energy delivery (Horsepower)
Cricket's chirp		1×10^{-6}
Burning match		1×10^{-2}
Man pumping	13	0.08
Man turning winch	18	0.10
Draft horse	120	1.00
Overshot 18-foot waterwheel		2–5
Windmill		2–8
Early steam engines		7–100
The *Queen Elizabeth*		246,000
Niagara Hydroelectric Plant		2,620,000
Earth receives from the sun		4×10^{15}

etc. A conservative estimate of power costs in the United States shows that 1.1 cents will buy 1 horsepower of electrical energy for 1 hour. (If desired, at least 90 per cent of this electrical energy can be transformed into mechanical energy.) Using these numbers one finds that an hour's pay of an unskilled worker will buy the equivalent work output of something in excess of 3000 men. These simple calculations account for the plight of the unskilled worker far more graphically than any number of books filled with labor force statistics.

Each second of each day we humans spend a tremendous amount of energy—in fact we spend it as if there were no tomorrow. In this section we take a brief look at how much man has been changing his spending habits and what he has left to spend. At this point the reader might feel compelled to call us up short by reminding us that he now knows (after reading Chapter 3) that energy is conserved so there is no need to worry about spending our energy reserves. Until we examine the second law in later chapters, all we can tell the reader is that while the quantity of energy is conserved, the quality of energy is not. One thousand calories at a high temperature is worth a lot more to man than 1000 calories at room temperature.

In examining our energy reserves and expenditures it will be useful to use a large energy unit to avoid writing out large numbers. The unit we shall use is called the Q and is defined as being equal to 10^{18} (a billion billion) British thermal units or 3.92×10^{14} horsepower-hours.

Mankind is believed to have used about 15 Q during the past 2000 years, with nearly half of this total being used within the past 100 years. Figure 4-4 illustrates this dramatic growth in world energy use and its projected future increase. When did man start to send this curve into its exponential climb? Some mark the time as shortly after he left the stagnation of the Dark Ages. Some even point to the year 1698 when Thomas Savery, a member of a well-known Devonshire family, was granted a patent on a condensing steam engine. Savery's engine had human-operated valves and though it never succeeded as a mine pump, the purpose for which it was designed, it was useful for other tasks.

Even with rapid industrialization, the world in 1850 was only spending about 0.01 Q per year. By 1950 the expenditure rate was about 0.1 Q per year—a tenfold increase in 100 years; during that

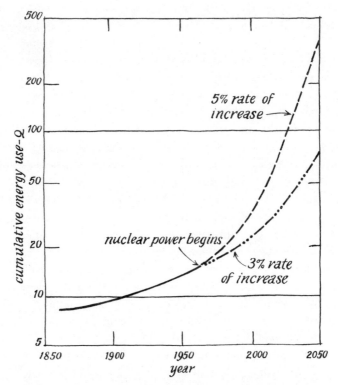

Figure 4–4. Probable cumulative world energy demands during the next 100 years. The energy demand is given in units of Q defined as 10^{18} Btu. The probable energy demand is shown for the two reasonable rates of increase: 3 per cent and 5 per cent.

same time period the world's population only doubled. Taking into account increasing industrialization and population growth, by the year 2050 the world will have spent between 75 Q (3 per cent rate of increase) and 275 Q (5 per cent rate of increase). The United States now accounts for about 40 per cent (0.05 Q in 1966) of the world's energy expenditure with only 6 per cent of the world's population.

The people of the world obtain their energy from the sources indicated in Figure 4–5. While about 50 per cent of the energy needs of the world are met by coal, it is interesting to note that wood fuel and farm waste (both animal and vegetable) supply almost 15 per cent of the world's energy needs. Though interest in and publicity about nuclear-fueled power plants has been widespread in the last ten years, a large part of the world knows no

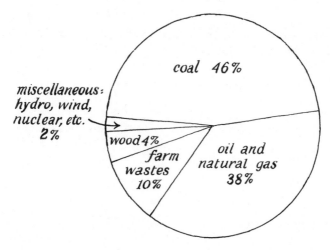

Figure 4–5. Present uses of energy capital and energy income. Eighty-five per cent of the world's present energy needs are supplied from capital reserves.

other way of cooking food and heating dwellings than the age-old method of burning animal dung.

The world's energy resources may be classified conveniently into two groups, called *energy capital* and *energy income*. Energy capital consists of fossil fuels, including coal, oil, and natural gas, which were created several hundred million years ago. In effect they represent solar energy that was stored in the form of chemical energy by the action of living organisms. Energy storage of this type is no longer taking place at a rate or on a scale to be of interest to man before he becomes extinct. We therefore come to the sad conclusion that sooner or later all of the fossil fuels of the world will have been used. Because fossil fuels are distributed unevenly around the world, some countries will feel the shortage before others. Estimates in this area are not very reliable but we believe that the data in the accompanying table are fair approximations of the actual fossil fuel energy reserves of the world. In computing the data for this table it was necessary to take into account the increased production cost that would be tolerable under conditions of scarcity.

**Estimated * Energy Content of World Reserves and
Resources of Fossil Fuels**

		known reserves †	additional potential resources †
Coal and peat		24.7	53.6
Liquid hydrocarbons (crude oil and natural gas liquids)		2.0	27.7
Natural gas		0.7	7.6
Oil shale and tar sands		—	13.1**
	Totals	27.4	102.0

* From B. C. Netschert and G. O. G. Lof, "New Sources of Energy in World Energy Economy," *Proceeding of the United Nations Conference on New Sources of Energy, General Sessions*, I (1963) (*United Nations Publications Sales* No. 63.1.2).
† In units of $Q = 10^{18}$ Btu.
** Known to exist but not economically feasible to utilize at present.

How long will this tremendous reservoir of energy from the past last us? The answer to this question depends on several factors. The "reserves" listed in the above table refer to resources known to exist; this stored energy can be used with present technology and under current economic conditions. On the other hand, the "resources" listed above include natural stocks whose utilization may or may not be technically or economically feasible. The resources are "potential" in that their future availability is hypothetical. In order to make some calculations let us assume that half of the additional potential resources can be made available economically. This gives us a total fossil fuel reserve of about 78 Q. If we are willing to assume that the world will go on spending energy from fossil fuel at the present rate of about 0.12 Q per year, we find that our fossil fuel reserves could keep us happy for about 650 years. However, to assume that the world's energy appetite will not increase in the face of the widespread industrialization we are now witnessing is ridiculous. We now borrow a trick from our banker friends and use the principle of compound interest to take into account our increasing energy appetite.[2] If we assume only a modest 3 per cent per year increase in demand for energy, then our fossil fuel reserves will last only about 100 years. If we assume a more realistic 5 per cent per year increase in demand for energy, then the world's fossil fuel reserves will last only about 80 years. These calculations assume that all of our energy requirements will be filled solely by fossil fuel. To lengthen this time before our fossil fuels are all used, it is necessary to level off our energy consumption (unlikely) or develop new energy sources.

Nuclear fuels will certainly play an increasingly important role in filling the world's energy demands. However, nuclear fuels used in fission or atom-splitting power plants must also be counted as energy capital. Estimates of nuclear energy reserves are difficult to make because it is possible to upgrade certain materials (thorium and uranium 238) by use of breeder reactors. In general, material which is breedable into useful nuclear fuels is many times more plentiful than naturally occurring fissionable

[2] *Josh Billings understood this principle well: "I don't know of anything more remorseless on the face of the earth than 7 per cent interest. It has no rest, nor no religion; it works nights and Sundays, and even wet days."*

fuel materials such as uranium 235. The best estimates presently available indicate that known reserves of uranium and thorium throughout the world are sufficient to supply the necessary energy —even with the anticipated rise in use—for about 500 years. Great Britain, which already has a scarcity of fossil fuels, has begun a program of building a network of nuclear-fuel central power stations.

Nuclear power has two disadvantages that are yet to be overcome. One is the problem of the safe disposal of radioactive wastes that nuclear power plants produce.[3] Another is that at present nuclear power is mostly confined to central power stations, since a convenient and safe means of making appreciable quantities of such power portable to any extent is lacking. This eliminates consideration of nuclear power for most types of transportation.

The problem of creating a sustained and controlled nuclear fusion reaction remains to be solved. In this reaction, which is the basis of the life-destroying hydrogen bomb and the life-giving sun, heavy hydrogen nuclei are united. This reaction represents the ultimate primary source of energy—nearly unlimited in extent with no radioactive wastes.

Water power is the major source of energy income utilized today. It contributes about 1 per cent of the world's energy needs and about 4 per cent of the energy used in the United States. However, this 4 per cent represents one-fifth of the electricity generated in the United States and at that we are using only 30

---

[3] *Some wags have suggested filling empty beer cans with the stuff, placing the beer cans in abandoned autos, and launching the autos into space, thereby simultaneously eliminating from the earth three troublesome artifacts of our civilization. But space rockets require a lot of energy, so thermodynamicists must regard this as prohibitively expensive in something more important than money.*

per cent of our hydroelectric potential of 80 million horsepower. The world's total hydroelectric power potential is estimated to be about ten times the present installed capacity. Even if all of this were used, the percentage contribution to the total world energy demand would remain small owing to the rapid increase in this demand.

The sun releases energy at a rate of about a million Q every 3 seconds. It has been estimated that about 5000 Q reach the earth every year. If we could harness but a small amount of this energy, man's energy supply problem would certainly be solved. We now utilize very little of this energy directly—chiefly because the energy reaches us in such diffuse form. A solar energy converter of 10 per cent efficiency requires about 110 square feet of collector area to produce 1 horsepower.

In a few instances man is able to reclaim part of the solar energy that strikes the earth. The sun evaporates water from the oceans, which subsequently falls as rain into rivers and reservoirs. The water trapped in the reservoirs is then allowed to run through hydraulic turbines to produce electricity. Man has also constructed solar batteries that turn sunlight directly into electricity but these have been used almost exclusively on satellites. Even before giant hydroelectric plants were built, some of the energy of the sun was reclaimed by man by way of windmills. The windmill simply recovers the energy stored by the sun in the giant convection currents we call the wind. Current world estimates, however, show that man puts more energy into electric fans than he receives from windmills.

Certainly one of the major factors that limits the use of energy is its cost. In the following table we list the number of cents it takes to purchase 1 horsepower for 1 hour from several sources. This table is presented for scaling purposes only, since the cost of even one energy source often varies considerably within a given country.

The natural fuels such as oil, natural gas, wood, coal, and gaso-

Cost of Energy in Various Forms

source of energy	cents/horsepower-hour
Fuel oil	0.3
Natural gas ⎫	
Wood ⎬	0.4
Coal ⎭	
Gasoline	0.65
Electricity (central station)	1.5
Sugar ⎫	
Bread ⎬	7.5
Butter ⎭	
Martini ($4\frac{27}{32}$ parts gin to $1\frac{5}{32}$ parts vermouth)	376
Flashlight battery	750
Caviar	925

line are seen to be the cheapest. If a source of energy is conveniently packaged, the price is affected, as witnessed by the cost of flashlight battery energy. If a source of energy is considered to be a rare and tasty treat, the price is affected, as witnessed by the cost of caviar. If the source of energy is considered dangerous or evil (or capable of inducing pleasant feelings in the user), the price is affected, as witnessed by the cost of martinis.

It should also be noted that whereas natural fuels are the most economical in providing heat as such, an energy source such as electricity may be very competitive if the energy is to be used in the form of work rather than heat because of a fundamental limitation on converting heat to work. This limitation, which applies only to the conversion of heat to work and not to the reverse case, constitutes the second law of thermodynamics—a subject we treat in detail in subsequent chapters.

How do these concepts about energy apply to the myriad devices and systems that constitute the technological environment in which we live? In the next few pages we see what the first law can tell us about a few of man's creations.

We live in an extremely mobile world; this can be made clear from energy considerations alone. We have about 100 million vehicles on the road in the United States; assume that each vehicle on the average has a 100 horsepower engine in it. In the terms of a central station engineer this comes to 10 billion horsepower of installed capacity:

$$100 \times 10^6 \text{ vehicles} \times 10^2 \frac{\text{horsepower}}{\text{vehicle}} = 10 \times 10^9 \text{ horsepower}$$

All of the electricity-generating plants in the world—steam, hydro, and internal combustion engine—have an installed capacity of "only" about 1×10^9 horsepower. That is to say, we have in the motor vehicles in the United States ten times more horsepower available to us than is available in all the electricity-generating plants of the entire world. Where does that energy go?

One of the peculiarities of the automobile is that only a small fraction of the energy of combustion of gasoline is actually used to accomplish the basic transportation task. As shown in Figure 4–6, about 75 per cent of the energy of combustion is lost as heat

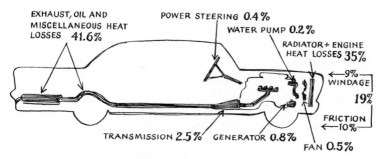

Figure 4–6. Where the energy goes in a medium-size automobile using a 120 horsepower engine to cruise at 50 miles per hour.

from the engine, the radiator, and the exhaust. The actual power requirement for a 4000-pound automobile is rather small under most conditions. When driving at a steady speed, part of the energy is used to overcome the friction between the road and the tires and the balance is required to overcome air friction. There are also minor power requirements for control, safety and passenger comfort. Thus when the first law is applied to the 120-horsepower engine [4] moving a 4000-pound car at 50 miles per hour, we find that only about 24 horsepower goes into moving the load. (When we say "applying the first law," we mean simply making sure that the energy supplied by the engine is accounted for.) The over-all efficiency of the automobile is about 20 per cent, which is not a very impressive figure in view of our dwindling hydrocarbon fuel reserves.

In 1962 we poured 59.3×10^9 gallons of gasoline into our vehicles. If we were to fill Africa's Zambesi River with this quantity of gasoline, it would take nearly two days (at 25 million gallons per minute) to dump it over Victoria Falls.

The efficiency with which electricity is generated in central station power plants presents a somewhat brighter picture.

The rate at which energy must be put into an electrical power generation plant by means of the combustion of coal, gas, or oil has steadily decreased. In 1925 it was necessary to burn 1.8 pounds of coal (6300 kilocalories of thermal energy) to obtain 1 kilowatt-hour of electricity; fifteen years later it took only 1.18 pounds of coal (4130 kilocalories) to get the same output. By 1962 the average power plant in the United States required only 0.76 pounds of coal (2660 kilocalories) to produce a kilowatt-hour of electricity. The most efficient plant in the United States in

[4] *That horsepower rating might sound low to American car buyers, but advertising copywriters have a different way of computing horsepower than do engineers. To each his own.*

that year, the Eddystone Station at Chester, Pennsylvania, required only 0.62 pounds of coal (2160 kilocalories) input to
deliver a kilowatt-hour of output. This corresponds to converting
39.8 per cent of the input thermal energy to electricity.

Several factors have influenced the capital cost of power plants
and the cost of fueling such plants. In general, power plant size
has increased until the limiting factor on the construction of individual turbine generators is simply the ability to ship turbine
shafts and generator rotors to the power plant location. One of
the largest steam-electric plants in the United States is the TVA
Widow Creek Station with a generating capacity of 1,750,000
kilowatts in eight units.

In 1956 coal-fired plant construction costs were estimated to be
$150–$200 per kilowatt of generating capacity, while the Atomic
Energy Commission estimated that a nuclear-fueled plant would
cost $300–$400 per kilowatt of capacity. In 1964 it was announced
that the 640,000 kilowatt Oyster Creek, New Jersey, nuclear
station would have an installed cost of $110 per kilowatt; in the
same year it was announced that the 1,230,000 kilowatt coal-fired
station at Brilliant, Ohio, would have an installed cost of only $97
per kilowatt of capacity. No doubt increased plant and unit sizes
have contributed substantially to these cost reductions, but the
recently uncovered price-fixing machinations of major utility
equipment suppliers are also a factor in the reduced installation
costs.

Though electric power generating plants have steadily grown in
size, man has found ways to release even larger amounts of energy in a controlled and orderly fashion. In the first Super Titan
rocket, 500 tons of solid propellant were burned in 90 seconds in
the first-stage boosters. This corresponds to an energy release
rate of about 5.5 million kilocalories per second. We may compare
this with the largest steam-generating boiler of contemporary
design which burns 10,500 tons of coal per day, yielding an average energy release of 0.6 million kilocalories per second. Thus

the rocket releases energy at nearly ten times the rate of the largest boiler, but for only 90 seconds.

A considerable part of the energy utilized in the world today goes into heating and cooling the buildings in which we live and work. This is nowhere more true than in the United States where many people now expect every place they go, including their automobiles, to be 72°F the year round.

In the last few years the electric utility industry has been trying to convince the American public that the best way to maintain this 72°F in winter is to dissipate electricity in high resistance wires inside the house. From a conservationist's point of view this is indefensible, since even in the best electric generating plants, 60 per cent of the fuel energy—whatever that fuel may be—is wasted. However, there is a way to utilize electricity in residential heating that is considerably more efficient than resistance heating and that demonstrates clearly an interesting application of the first law.

The heat pump takes heat from a relatively low temperature source and delivers it to a region at a higher temperature. Let us consider a heat pump as it is applied in heating a house that we wish to maintain at 72°F even when the outside temperature may fall to 0°F. The type of heat pump we consider consists of four essential parts, as shown in Figure 4–7a: two heat exchangers, a compressor, and an expansion valve. We also require an inexpensive energy reservoir at a relatively low temperature. In our design we assume that we have buried one of our heat exchangers in a well that contains water at a temperature of 50°F (in the Chicago area a well 60 feet deep will supply water at about 50°F all year).

The working fluid in a heat pump, as in a refrigerator, is generally a chemical refrigerant such as Freon. The pump compresses the Freon to a high pressure and at the same time raises its temperature during the compression process from 40° to 90°F. The

Freon is then supplied to the heat exchanger located in the duct-work in the house where a fan blows air over the pipes containing the hot Freon; as the air passes over the pipes, it is warmed and the Freon is cooled to 75°F. The high pressure Freon then flows through an expansion valve, which can be simply a short section of small diameter pipe. As it passes through this restriction in the line and then into some large diameter pipe, it expands. This

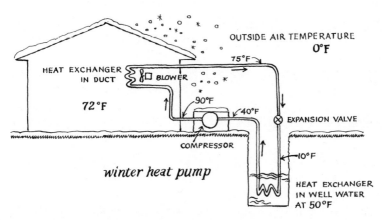

Figure 4-7a. In winter electrical power is used to pump energy out of the low temperature well water up to a temperature where it is suitable for heating a house. This scheme is called a *heat pump.*

larger diameter pipe is maintained at a low pressure because it is connected to the low pressure side of the compressor. The expansion of the Freon from high pressure to low pressure causes its temperature to fall to about 10°F. This low temperature, low pressure Freon is now led into the heat exchanger in the well water where the 50°F well water heats up the Freon to 40°F. In this process heat flows from the well water to the Freon. The 40°F Freon now passes back to the compressor and the cycle begins again.

In this heat pumping device the compressor has raised the low-temperature energy picked up in the well to a level where it may be used to heat the house. Energy is added to the working fluid at two places in the cycle: (1) in the compressor as it is raised from low to high pressure, and (2) in the well water where it is raised from a low to a high temperature. Energy is removed from the working fluid as it passes through the heat exchanger in the house ducts. When the first law is applied to this kind of steady-flow device, it says that the net work done (W) must equal the net heat transfer to the Freon (Q) or:

$$W_{\text{compressor}} = Q_{\text{from the well}} - Q_{\text{to the house}}$$

The cost of heating a house using this heat pump would be about one-third to one-fourth the cost of heating the house by electricity alone, because in this scheme electricity is used merely to "pump" the heat from the temperature of the cool well water up to a higher temperature.

One of the most attractive features of a heat pump is that the flow of the working fluid can be reversed and the same unit used to cool the house in summer. Under these circumstances, illustrated in Figure 4–7b, the Freon leaves the compressor at 90°F, flows to the well where it is cooled by the well water to 70°F; it then crosses the expansion valve where the sudden reduction in pressure causes its temperature to drop to 55°F in which state it is now in a suitable condition for reducing the temperature of the air as it flows across the ductwork in the house. The working fluid then returns to the compressor where it is pumped back up to a high pressure and the cycle starts again. In this case electrical power is used to pump heat out of the house and into the well. (The household refrigerator does the same thing when it pumps heat out of the food compartment into the kitchen.)

You will notice that exactly the same equipment is used in both summer and winter. One of the biggest drawbacks in the use of such equipment has been the high installation costs associated

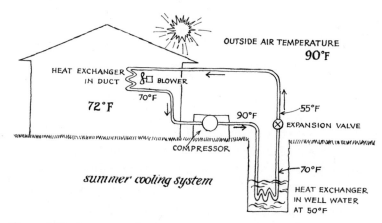

OUTSIDE AIR TEMPERATURE
90°F

HEAT EXCHANGER
IN DUCT   BLOWER

72°F
70°F

90°F   55°F

EXPANSION VALVE

COMPRESSOR

summer cooling system

70°F

HEAT EXCHANGER
IN WELL WATER
AT 50°F

Figure 4–7b. In summer electrical power is used to pump energy out of a warm house to cool it. Note that the same equipment can be used summer and winter.

with the equipment located outside the house. Burying pipe in the earth or pumping up well water to be used in the outside heat exchanger have proved to be expensive jobs.

Man spends the energy available to him in so many different ways that the number is almost uncountable. However, we may now say with certainty that he is spending more and more of his energy on the production of freshwater from seawater. In some ways it is too bad that we have not found more uses for seawater—it is 2700 times more plentiful than freshwater.

To say that there is no shortage of freshwater might seem paradoxical in light of the statements of the preceding paragraph. Nevertheless, it is true. The total rainfall on land areas is more than ample to supply man's needs: it is estimated to be about 26,000 gallons per day (gpd) for every inhabitant on earth. The problem is one of distribution; some areas have more than they can possibly use (Mount Waialeale on the island of Kauai in Hawaii has an average annual rainfall in excess of 470 inches) while other areas have little or no rainfall for several years at a time.

Perhaps the most obvious answer to local shortages is simply to ship water from where it is plentiful to where it is scarce, which is being done in some places. For example, large quantities of water are pumped from northern California to southern California. But this costs energy and thus money too—from 5 to 15 cents per 1000 gallons for each 100 miles.

Man's water needs are rather modest in comparison with the total supply available. Average per capita consumption in the United States is 1650 gpd as shown below:

> 750 gallons per day for agriculture
> 750 gallons per day for industrial use
> 150 gallons per day for household use

It requires 275 tons of water to make 1 ton of steel (and there is a ton of steel or more in the average auto), while it takes 20 gallons of water to refine 1 gallon of petroleum.

If shipping costs become prohibitive (and in most cases this happens when the distance involved is greater than 500 miles), we look in other directions to alleviate the problem. Many countries that need freshwater have thousands of miles of seacoast and hence the raw material is available. What is required to turn this raw material into freshwater?

The answer is energy, and the equipment needed to utilize that energy. We list energy first because there are many different types of equipment that may be utilized in desalination, but all require energy to make them operate. These two items, the energy and the equipment, determine the cost of the water produced by a plant. A fact well known to engineers, but frequently overlooked by those not used to working with this type of problem, is that as one tries to decrease the energy requirements for a process, the fixed costs on the investment (equipment) are almost inevitably increased. Frequently the job of process design engineers is to determine the optimum balance between these two conflicting forces.

A substantial amount of energy is required to extract water from a salt solution, or to put it more familiarly, to divide a salt solution into freshwater and a more concentrated salt solution commonly called brine. In general, separation processes require expenditure of energy. For example, air contains about 20 per cent oxygen; if we desire pure oxygen, we must spend energy (money) to get it. So it is with seawater; if we wish to obtain freshwater, it is necessary to concentrate a salt solution (make it more salty) and thus we must spend energy. The concepts involved in this type of problem are most easily handled by the use of entropy, a subject we discuss in later chapters.

The less freshwater we wish to get from a given amount of seawater, the less energy we must spend to obtain the freshwater. The limiting case of zero recovery—a very small amount of freshwater from a very large amount of seawater—has been calculated to require 2.98 kilowatt-hours per 1000 gallons of freshwater. As the per cent recovery goes up, the work required to achieve the recovery also goes up. Reliable estimates indicate that large-scale plants can be constructed that will require about 30 kilowatt-hours to provide 1000 gallons of desalinated water. Although this is an efficiency of only 10 per cent compared with the ideal, no breakthroughs have appeared on the horizon to offer a dramatic improvement.

There are many techniques and phenomena that may be used to obtain freshwater from seawater. The one that is the most widely used is a distillation or evaporation process. Distillation is also the process nature uses to produce freshwater from the oceans in the form of clouds by utilizing the energy in sunlight. Small ocean-going units used on ships and large land-based units (up to 3 million gpd) using distillation have been built.

In the distillation process heat is supplied to cause freshwater to boil away from the saltwater; the heat is generally supplied by means of steam that condenses (giving up its latent heat) in pipes submerged in the seawater. The vapor so obtained can be condensed to freshwater.

However, the first law tells us that if the distillation is carried out in only one stage, not more than 1 pound of evaporated freshwater can be obtained per pound of steam. The resulting energy cost alone would make water produced in such a plant far too expensive. For a distillation plant to be economically practical, the energy now stored in the freshwater vapor must be utilized. In principle this may be done by leading the vapor to another tank where it is used to evaporate more water. Let us consider the example illustrated in Figure 4–8. Steam at 250°F is condensed in a tank of boiling seawater at 220°F. The 220°F freshwater vapor is led to another tank of seawater where its energy is used to evaporate water at 210°F. It is necessary to maintain the second tank at a lower pressure than the first so that its contents will boil at 210°F, but this is not difficult to achieve. The water evaporated in the second stage is now used to evaporate water in a third stage at a temperature of 200°F, and so on. Such a scheme is known as a multiple-effect evaporation plant. It is possible to obtain yields of 8 to 10 pounds of freshwater per pound of steam. Current work indicates that the optimum number of stages lies between 10 and 20.

Considerable attention has been given to combined electrical power plants and desalination plants fueled by nuclear reactors. Every power plant that uses heat to produce electricity must throw away a large part (at least 60 per cent in current plants) of the heat released by the energy source. That is, so far we have not been able to convert more than about 40 per cent of the combustion or nuclear fission energy into electrical energy or work. This is a consequence of the second law of thermodynamics, which is discussed in later chapters. It has now been realized that this low temperature thermal energy need not be completely wasted. It is, in fact, almost ideal for use in distillation desalination plants.

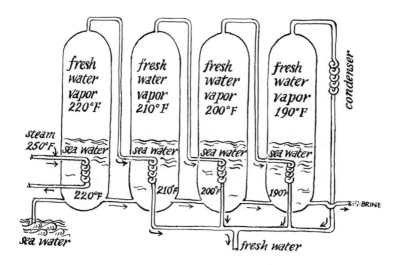

Figure 4–8. Four-stage freshwater distillation plant.

Large-scale thermal reactors are now being designed to produce electricity and freshwater at combined costs for power and water heretofore believed to be impossible. The plants now being considered are large; they will be capable of producing more than 190 megawatts of electrical energy and the exhaust steam from the electrical portion of the plant will yield 170 million gpd of freshwater.

Man is now looking for freshwater everywhere. One scheme that has been proposed to obtain freshwater would, it appears to us, open new avenues of recreation. The plan is simple enough: tow icebergs from the polar regions and melt them in drydocks in the temperate regions. If this scheme is ever realized, then watching icebergs melt might become as popular a spectator sport as observing submarine races.

chapter five
the chemical c.p.a.

"Why think? Why not try the experiment?" is a remark attributed to John Hunter, an eighteenth-century British anatomist and surgeon. It is only a modest exaggeration to say that some theoreticians hold a perfectly opposite opinion, namely, that if something has to be established in the laboratory it is hardly worth establishing. In this chapter we adopt a middle course, which consists of describing some experiments and measurements that have been done and showing how these results can be used with some thinking in deducing the results of other experiments. Our particular concern is with chemical reactions.

As a first step in our consideration of chemical reactions we restate part of the first law in these terms: *The difference between the energy of a system in state A and the energy of the system in state B does not depend on how the system gets from state A to state B or vice versa.* In mathematical language, we would say the same thing in these words: *Energy is a state function.*[1] This

---

[1] *In thermodynamics we commonly encounter two kinds of functions:* state functions *such as energy and* path functions *such as heat and work. The meanings of state and path functions can be illustrated by means of a geographical example. A traveler going from London to New York goes west by a certain number of degrees, which can be calculated by subtracting the longitude of one city from that of the other. The number of degrees one city is west of another depends on the longitudes of the two cities but not on how one travels from one city to the other. Although New York is a fixed number of degrees west of London, the miles traveled by an airplane in going from one city to the other depends on the path or route of the airplane. We say that "degrees west" is a*

last statement means that the energy of a system depends only on the state of the system, not on the history or future of the system. With a little thought, we can proceed from these statements and the first law to ideas and methods that are directly applicable to a huge variety of chemical processes.

Everyone recognizes that careful consideration of energy changes associated with combustion is important to the man who is trying to decide whether coal or natural gas is the most economical fuel for a given purpose. The same scientific principles derived from the first law are also applied in much the same way to evaluating potential rocket fuels and deciding that potatoes are more fattening than steaks. But these are not the only interesting and useful applications of the first law to chemical systems. We can also apply the first law to gain understanding of the structures of molecules and the forces that hold the atoms together in these molecules. Now on to the thinking that must precede application of the first law.

In Chapter 3 we wrote the first law as $E_2 - E_1 = Q - W$, with the subscripts 2 and 1 indicating the final and initial states while Q and W represent heat absorbed and work done. As we have already pointed out, energy is a state function. But heat and work are not state functions. The work involved in a process depends on how that process is carried out as well as on the initial and final states. Almost everyone has said sometime that some kind of manual labor can be done either the easy way or the hard way. Similarly, the heat involved can depend on the details of how the process is carried out.

The kind of work to be considered here is what we call mechani-

---

state function and "miles traveled" is a path function. The first depends only on the two locations considered, while the second also depends on how one gets from one city to the other.

cal work.[2] This mechanical work often takes the form of work that is done by the system in moving a piston against a restraining pressure. But when the piston is locked in place so that the volume is constant, the system does not accomplish work on the surroundings nor do the surroundings do any work on the system. Thus $W = 0$ and $E_2 - E_1 = Q$ for processes taking place at constant volume. It may help here to consider a man pushing against a solid wall. No matter how hard he pushes, the wall refuses to move and he accomplishes no thermodynamic work because even a large force times zero distance equals zero work done. Since our nonworking man does expend energy, which appears entirely in the form of heat, he can get as tired by pushing against a wall as he can by pushing a wheelbarrow loaded with bricks. The important point to note here is that $\Delta E = Q$ for all constant volume processes, with all energy changes appearing solely as heat that is transferred between the system and the surroundings.

Most chemical processes and also biological processes take place at constant pressure rather than at constant volume. Such processes are equivalent to processes taking place in a cylinder closed at one end with a piston on which a constant external pressure is pushing. This constant pressure usually is the ordinary atmospheric pressure, which amounts to 14.7 pounds per square inch or is equivalent to the pressure exerted at the bottom of a column of mercury that is 76 centimeters high.

[2] *Most thermodynamicists make a big deal out of defining work; we won't. Mark Twain's definition that "Work consists of whatever a body is obliged to do, and play consists of whatever a body is not obliged to do" is surely correct in a personal sense but does present thermodynamic difficulties. It is sufficient here to say that thermodynamic work can be defined in terms of a force times a distance through which the force acts and can thus be reduced to terms of lifting or falling weights.*

So long as the external pressure is constant, the work done by the system on the surroundings amounts to the pressure times the change in volume, as expressed by [3]

$$W = P(V_2 - V_1)$$

If the second volume is greater than the initial volume so that $(V_2 - V_1)$ is positive, W is also positive and work has been done by the system on the surroundings. On the other hand, the second volume may be less than the initial volume so that $(V_2 - V_1)$ and W are negative, indicating that the surroundings have accomplished work on the system.

As our initial step in applying the first law to constant pressure processes we put $W = P(V_2 - V_1)$ into $E_2 - E_1 = Q - W$ to obtain

$$E_2 - E_1 = Q - P(V_2 - V_1)$$

Recognizing that the last part of this expression can be written as $(PV_2 - PV_1)$, we can solve for Q and then arrange the terms in the answer so that we have

$$Q = (E_2 + PV_2) - (E_1 + PV_1)$$

[3] *Since pressure is force divided by area as in* $P = f/A$, *we also have*

$$f = P \times A$$

Work has been defined as force times distance. In this case the relevant distance is the height (h) *through which the force is moved, so we have*

$$W = f \times h = P \times A \times h$$

Recognizing that the cross-sectional area of a cylinder times the height gives the change in volume in the cylinder, we arrive at

$$V_2 - V_1 = A \times h$$

and thence the expression

$$W = P(V_2 - V_1)$$

We could, if we wished, proceed to use this and other expressions involving $(E + PV)$, but to avoid unnecessary awkwardness we adopt the letter H as a shorthand expression for $(E + PV)$ and use the name *enthalpy* for the quantity

$$H = (E + PV)$$

Now our expression for Q becomes simply

$$Q = H_2 - H_1 \text{ or } Q = \Delta H$$

Because of this last equality, it is common to speak of the *enthalpy* as *the heat*. This expression is only correct for processes that take place at constant pressure, but it is those processes that presently interest us.

Earlier in this chapter we pointed out that energy is a state function or property. Enthalpy is also a state function since it depends only on the state functions energy, pressure, and volume. We shall make use of the fact that enthalpy is a state function, which means that the change in enthalpy for a process, represented by $H_2 - H_1$ or more commonly by ΔH, depends on the initial and final states but not at all upon the path between those states. Incidentally, it might be noted that the enthalpy is a state function whether or not the pressure is constant, but $\Delta H = Q$ only when the initial pressure equals the final pressure.

As one last preliminary to the application of the first law to chemical reactions, we must explain some chemical terminology. Almost every reader of this book will already know that H_2O and $NaCl$ are chemical abbreviations for water and common table salt. Similar abbreviations may be written for other substances. But the expression H_2O may also be used as a symbol to represent a molecule of water. This symbol tells us that each molecule of water is made up of two atoms of hydrogen and one atom of oxygen. Similarly, the symbol O_2 for oxygen tells us that molecules of oxygen consist of two atoms.

Because atoms and molecules are so very tiny, any reasonably ordinary chemical reaction involves many molecules. It is therefore also common to use H_2O, O_2, and the like as symbols to represent a large number of molecules of water, oxygen, or some other substance. A convenient counting unit for doughnuts is the dozen, and the symbol Dn might represent 12 doughnuts. A gross is a convenient counting unit for some other items. For instance, we might take Pc as a "chemical" symbol for 144 paper clips. But numbers such as 12 or 144 or even the national debt expressed in pennies are entirely too small to be convenient counting units for atoms and molecules, so we use *Avogadro's number* for the counting unit in chemistry. This number is 602,000,000,000,000,000,-000,000, which is more conveniently written as 6.02×10^{23}, where 10^{23} indicates that the decimal point is to be moved 23 places to the right. We identify counting units of 12 and 144 as a dozen and a gross; similarly, we identify the counting unit of 6.02×10^{23} as a *mole*. Thus we use H_2O as a symbol to represent one mole of water molecules.

Now that we have defined a mole to be a particular counting unit, we may make use of tables of atomic weights, more properly called atomic masses. These atomic masses have been chosen so that the tabulated numbers correspond to the masses, expressed in grams, of one mole of the various chemical elements. For example, the atomic mass of carbon is listed as 12. Thus 12 grams of carbon consist of 6.02×10^{23} atoms of carbon. The atomic mass of oxygen is listed as 16. This means that one mole of oxygen *atoms* has a mass of 16 grams. Oxygen ordinarily consists of molecules containing two atoms each, as indicated by the symbol O_2. Thus one mole of oxygen atoms gives us only one-half mole of oxygen molecules. Or we might say that the mass of one mole of oxygen molecules represented by O_2 is $2 \times 16 = 32$ grams. One mole of O_2 molecules contains two moles of oxygen atoms.

As a shorthand expression for the combustion of carbon in oxygen to yield carbon dioxide we write

$$C + O_2 \rightarrow CO_2$$

This expression may be read "One mole of carbon reacts with one mole of oxygen molecules to yield one mole of carbon dioxide." Measurements made with calorimeters (calorie meter—see Figure 5–1 for an illustration) have shown that the heat evolved is 94,000 calories for each 12 grams of carbon that is burned. Since the quantities of heat involved in this and many other chemical

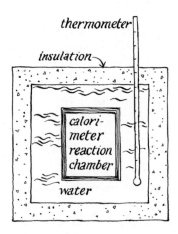

Figure 5–1. Schematic illustration of a calorimeter used for determination of heats of chemical reactions under constant volume conditions. In this case, ΔH is not equal to Q, but is derived from the measured Q, which is obtained from the observed temperature increase of the water surrounding the calorimeter reaction chamber. Calorimeters for investigation of reactions under constant pressure conditions are also used, particularly for reactions that take place in water solutions. A variety of means of measuring temperature changes (some sensitive to 10^{-6} degrees C) and of minimizing or controlling exchange of heat with the surroundings are used.

reactions are large, it is convenient to use the kilocalorie (1000 calories) as our unit of heat. Recognizing that 12 grams of carbon is 1 mole of carbon, we say that the heat evolved in this combustion reaction is 94 kilocalories per mole of carbon.

The 94 kcal (abbreviation for kilocalories) referred to above are evolved when the combustion reaction takes place at ordinary atmospheric constant pressure. Remembering that $Q = \Delta H$ for constant pressure processes and that Q is negative for processes that evolve heat, we see that $\Delta H = -94$ kcal for the combustion of 1 mole of carbon. Thus we write

$$C + O_2 \rightarrow CO_2 \qquad \Delta H = -94 \text{ kcal}$$

Studies of the heat of combustion of carbon monoxide (CO) are of value because gaseous carbon monoxide (often mixed with hydrogen and called water gas) has been used as a fuel. Appropriate calorimetric measurements have shown that the heat evolved on combustion of carbon monoxide is 68 kcal for each mole ($12 + 16 = 28$ grams) of carbon monoxide. All this is represented concisely by

$$CO + \tfrac{1}{2}O_2 \rightarrow CO_2 \qquad \Delta H = -68 \text{ kcal}$$

Note that $\tfrac{1}{2}O_2$ means that we are concerned with one-half mole of oxygen (3.01×10^{23} molecules or 16 grams).

Direct measurement of the heat of combustion of carbon in an inadequate supply of oxygen so that the product will be carbon monoxide is experimentally difficult. We therefore make use of the state function properties of the enthalpy to get the answer without doing laboratory work.

A diagram representing transformation in the carbon-carbon monoxide-carbon dioxide system is shown in Figure 5–2. Since enthalpy is a state function, we know that ΔH for going from C to CO_2 must be independent of the path. The one-step reaction of carbon with oxygen to produce carbon dioxide yields $\Delta H = -94$ kcal; consequently the two-step reaction by way of carbon monoxide must also yield a *total* $\Delta H = -94$ kcal. Since one of the two steps is already known to have $\Delta H = -68$ kcal, we deduce that the other step must have $\Delta H = -26$ kcal in order to make the total -94 kcal. Thus we have the following:

$$C + \tfrac{1}{2}O_2 \rightarrow CO \qquad \Delta H = -26 \text{ kcal}$$

The ideas behind the above calculations are not new. In 1780 Lavoisier and Laplace stated as a self-evident truth that as much heat is required to decompose a compound as is liberated when the compound is formed from its elements. This statement and its generalization to a statement that the heat involved in a reaction

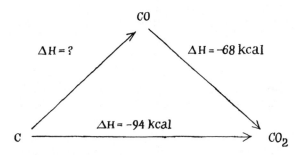

Figure 5-2. The cycle pictured here is consistent with the first law and the state function nature of enthalpy only if the unknown $\Delta H = -26$ kcal.

is equal to the sum of the heats associated with the steps that make up the whole reaction were both confirmed experimentally by W. G. Hess in 1840.

Although it is possible in principle to evaluate heats for a great variety of reactions by means of diagrams like that in Figure 5-2, the prospects are enough to make cowards out of bold men. The situation is much worse than merely working with many-sided figures. Many of the ΔH values that would be used in constructing the many-sided figures of interest would themselves have to be derived from many-sided figures, and some of the ΔH values in these figures would have come from other many-sided figures, etc. Further, merely tabulating and then indexing experimental ΔH values to be used in such calculations is not a trivial problem. But the way out of this forest of difficulties is as easy as understanding the heights of mountains and the depths of oceans.

How high is Pike's Peak? How deep is the bottom of the Mariana Trench in the Pacific Ocean? One answer might be that the top of Pike's Peak is 14,110 feet above sea level and that the bottom of the Mariana Trench is 36,200 feet below sea level. Or we might say that the height of Pike's Peak is +14,110 feet and that of the Mariana Trench is −36,200 feet. We have taken sea level as our zero point or reference for height. Heights of mountains and depths of depressions are illustrated on this basis in Figure

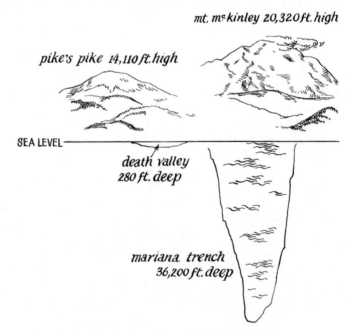

Figure 5–3. Illustration of the concept of a reference level.

5–3. It is easy to see from this diagram that simple arithmetic tells us how much higher one mountain is than another. For instance, the top of Mount McKinley is $20{,}320 - 14{,}110 = 6{,}210$ feet higher than the top of Pike's Peak. Similarly, the top of Mount McKinley is $(20{,}320) - (-280) = (20{,}320) + (280) = 20{,}600$ feet higher than the lowest point in Death Valley.

Since heights cannot be measured in any absolute way, but only have meaning in terms of some reference or zero level, all the figures above are based on the arbitrary but convenient choice of sea level as the reference height. Similarly, absolute values of the enthalpy H cannot be measured. Only changes or differences in enthalpy such as $H_2 - H_1 = Q$ can be measured and thus have real meaning. Therefore, if we want to tabulate and later use numerical values of enthalpies, we must choose an enthalpy reference analogous to the sea level reference chosen for heights of mountains and depths of valleys.

By general agreement the zero or reference level for enthalpy is taken to be each of the chemical elements in its ordinary stable state. Thus the enthalpies of carbon in the graphite form, zinc and copper in their ordinary solid forms, and oxygen, hydrogen, and nitrogen in their ordinary gaseous states represented by O_2, H_2, and N_2 are all taken to be zero.

We have already seen that $\Delta H = -94$ kcal for the reaction of 1 mole of carbon with oxygen to form carbon dioxide as indicated by

$$C + O_2 \rightarrow CO_2 \qquad \Delta H = -94 \text{ kcal}$$

Remembering that ΔH represents $H_2 - H_1$ or the enthalpy of the final state minus that of the initial state, we see that

$$-94 = H_{CO_2} - (H_C + H_{O_2})$$

Both H_C and H_{O_2}, which represent the enthalpies of carbon and oxygen, are zero according to our reference choice and therefore the enthalpy of CO_2 is $H_{CO_2} = -94$ kcal. In this way measured

ΔH values have been used for building great tables of enthalpies, with each tabulated value based on the reference choice of zero enthalpy for the elements in their standard states.

These enthalpies can be used in calculating ΔH values for chemical reactions much like a table of heights can be used in calculating changes in elevation in going from one mountain peak to another. A calculation of this sort is illustrated with Figure 5–4.

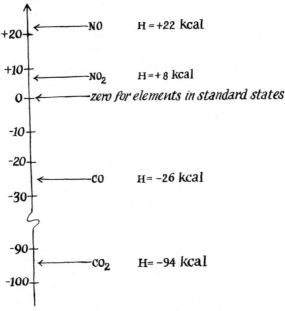

Figure 5–4. "Elevation" illustration of enthalpies. Going from CO to CO_2 as in $CO + \frac{1}{2}O_2 \rightarrow CO_2$ involves *descending* by 68 kcal, so $\Delta H = -68$ kcal for this reaction. Going from CO_2 to CO as $CO_2 \rightarrow CO + \frac{1}{2}O_2$ involves an *ascent* of 68 kcal, so $\Delta H = +68$ kcal. The first reaction evolves heat while the second absorbs heat.

The same principles apply to calculating ΔH for $CO + NO_2 \rightarrow CO_2 + NO$. The composite "elevation" of $CO_2 + NO$ is $-94 + 22 = -72$ kcal. The composite "elevation" of $CO + NO_2$ is $-26 + 8 = -18$ kcal. In going from -18 kcal to -72 kcal there is a *descent* of 54 kcal, so the reaction evolves heat and $\Delta H = -54$ kcal.

Knowledge of enthalpies permits easy calculation of $\Delta H = Q$ values for chemical reactions and is of value for several reasons. The most obvious applications of such calculations are in cases where the amount of heat associated with the reaction is of prime interest. An old-fashioned but still important example is the evaluation of fuels for space (of buildings, not outer) heating or providing energy for industrial processes. Exotic fuels for rocket engines are also evaluated partly on the basis of ΔH values for the reactions they undergo. Similarly, part of the evaluation of foodstuffs is based on ΔH values.

Other less obvious applications are also important. One of these involves combination of ΔH values with results derived from the second and third laws of thermodynamics. This combination, which is explained in Chapter 8, permits us to know the state of equilibrium in many chemical systems under many different conditions and thus to predict in advance the extent of various chemical reactions and processes under these conditions.

Another interesting application involves only the first law, so we can take it up now. From calculations of $\Delta H = Q$ values for appropriately chosen reactions it is possible to evaluate the average energies or strengths of the bonds holding the atoms to one another in chemical compounds.

As a first step in deducing bond strengths we evaluate ΔH for the following reaction: [4]

$$CH_4(g) \rightarrow C(g) + 4\,H(g) \qquad \Delta H = +397\,\text{kcal}$$

In this reaction equation CH_4 represents methane (principal component of natural gas), and C and H represent carbon and hydrogen. The symbol (g) is added to indicate that the preceding

[4] *Watch out!* H (*roman*) *stands for hydrogen, but* H (*italicized*) *means enthalpy.* ΔH *always means the change in enthalpy and equals Q in all cases of interest in this chapter.*

substances are in the gaseous state. We have also written H rather than the more usual H_2 because we are presently interested in atomic, rather than molecular, hydrogen as a product in this reaction. The ΔH value written above with the reaction equation was calculated from enthalpies of methane, *gaseous* carbon, and *atomic* hydrogen, each of these enthalpies being based on the "sea level" of *solid* carbon in the graphite form and *gaseous* hydrogen in the molecular form represented by H_2. This calculation is summarized in Figure 5–5.

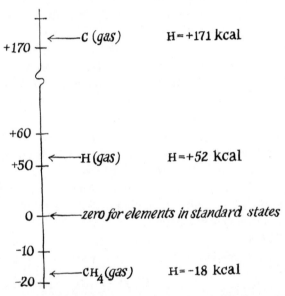

Figure 5–5. "Elevation" illustration of enthalpies. In going from $CH_4(g)$ at −18 kcal to $C(g) + 4\,H(g)$ at $171 + 4(52) = +379$ kcal there is an ascent of $379 + 18 = +397$ kcal, so heat is absorbed and $\Delta H = +397$ kcal for $CH_4(g) \rightarrow C(g) + 4\,H(g)$.

Interpretation of the above ΔH in terms of chemical bonds is suggested by rewriting the reaction equation to show the bonds in methane as lines connecting the bonded atoms as follows:

$$\begin{array}{c} \text{H} \\ | \\ \text{H--C--H}(g) \rightarrow \text{C}(g) + 4\,\text{H}(g) \qquad \Delta H = +397\,\text{kcal} \\ | \\ \text{H} \end{array}$$

The net effect of the reaction is the breaking of four bonds between carbon and hydrogen atoms, represented by C—H. According to the listed $\Delta H = 397$ kcal, breaking these bonds requires absorption of 397 kcal from the surroundings. The average energy required for breaking 1 mole of C—H bonds is therefore $397 \div 4 = 99$ kcal. Let us call this value the carbon-hydrogen or C—H bond energy, by which we mean an energy to be associated with 1 mole (6.02×10^{23}) of C—H bonds. This figure represents the average energy required to break 1 mole of C—H bonds or the average energy liberated as heat when 1 mole of· C—H bonds is formed from the separated atoms.

Next we make use of the same sort of calculation for ethane, C_2H_6. The decomposition of ethane into unbonded atoms of carbon and hydrogen is indicated by the following symbols:

$$\begin{array}{c} \text{H}\quad \text{H} \\ |\quad\ | \\ \text{H--C--C--H}(g) \rightarrow 2\,\text{C}(g) + 6\,\text{H}(g) \qquad \Delta H = +676\,\text{kcal} \\ |\quad\ | \\ \text{H}\quad \text{H} \end{array}$$

This reaction requires the absorption of 676 kcal for the decomposition of 1 mole of ethane. In this decomposition 6 moles of C—H bonds and 1 mole of C—C bonds are broken. The energy required for breaking the 6 moles of C—H bonds is $6 \times 99 = 594$ kcal, leaving $676 - 594 = 82$ kcal as the energy required to break 1 mole of C—C bonds. Similar calculations based on ΔH values for decomposition of other compounds into their constituent unbonded atoms lead to bond energy values for bonds between other elements.

We may also find bond energies for other kinds of bonds between the same elements. For instance, consideration of such compounds as ethylene, C_2H_4, or

$$\begin{array}{cc} H & H \\ | & | \\ H\text{—}C\!\!=\!\!C\text{—}H \end{array}$$

leads to a bond energy value for the $C\!\!=\!\!C$ double bond. In these pictures where a line represents a bond, we are using the line to represent a pair of electrons that is shared between the two atoms that are bonded. This pair of shared electrons acts in many ways like a tiny spring. When small amounts of energy are absorbed, the spring permits the bound atoms to vibrate with respect to each other, but when a sufficiently large amount of energy is absorbed, the spring is broken and the atoms fly apart. In some substances neighboring atoms share two or even three pairs of electrons and we say that such atoms are connected by double or triple bonds. The two carbon atoms in a molecule of ethylene share two pairs of electrons; consequently we say they are connected by a double bond represented by $C\!\!=\!\!C$. In acetylene of formula C_2H_2 or

$$H\text{—}C\!\!\equiv\!\!C\text{—}H$$

the carbon atoms share three pairs of electrons with each other and we say that they are connected by a triple bond. In acetone of formula C_3H_6O or

$$\begin{array}{ccc} H & O & H \\ | & \| & | \\ H\text{—}C\text{—}C\text{—}C\text{—}H \\ | & & | \\ H & & H \end{array}$$

the central carbon atom and the oxygen atom share two pairs of electrons and we say that there is a carbon-oxygen double bond represented by $C\!\!=\!\!O$.

Our evaluations of bond energies have implied that the strength of a given bond is independent of the nature of other bonds in the molecule under consideration. If this implication were exactly correct, we would be able to calculate exact ΔH values for decomposition of all molecules containing familiar bonds and would also obtain exactly the same bond energy values from different compounds. For instance, ΔH values for decomposition of acetone (formula already given) and acetic acid of formula

$$
\begin{array}{ccc}
\text{H} & \text{O} & \\
| & \| & \\
\text{H—C—C—O—H} \\
| & & \\
\text{H} & &
\end{array}
$$

would lead to identical values for the C=O double bond energy. It turns out that bond energies are almost, but not quite exactly, independent of neighboring bonds.

From consideration of ΔH values for decomposition of many compounds into unbonded atoms it has been possible to construct tables of average bond energy values. A short list of such bond energies is given in the following table.

Bond Energies (expressed in kcal per mole)

bond	bond energy	bond	bond energy
H—H	104	C—H	99
C—C	83	C—O	84
C=C	147	C=O	176
C≡C	200		

Studies of bond energies by Linus Pauling (two Nobel Prizes, one for chemistry in 1954 and one for peace in 1962) and others have contributed much to present understanding of the nature of chemical bonds. We consider only one important example, benzene.

In 1825 Michael Faraday discovered the substance that we now call benzene. A variety of experiments over the next fifty years established that the carbon atoms are arranged in a regular hexagon and that one hydrogen atom is bonded to each carbon atom.

But the very experiments, mostly carried out by nineteenth-century organic chemists in Germany, that confirmed the arrangement of the atoms in benzene seemed to provide conflicting and confusing information about the bonds between the atoms in benzene. These difficulties were largely unresolved from the middle of the nineteenth century until the application of quantum mechanics about 1930. The first and to date most useful way out of the difficulties concerning bonding in benzene (and many other molecules) was afforded by the "resonance theory" of which Linus Pauling was one of the chief architects.

According to this resonance theory, which is based on quantum mechanical calculations, the bonding structure of benzene can be described as a mixture or hybrid of the structures pictured in Figure 5–6. The word resonance is used because of a mathematical analogy to resonance of a system of pendulums and definitely does not mean that a molecule of benzene oscillates from one

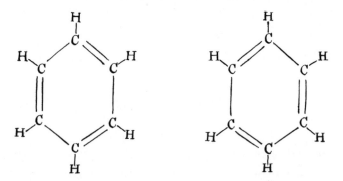

Figure 5–6. According to the resonance theory, the bonding structure of benzene is to be thought of as a hybrid of the two "parent" structures pictured here, in which each line represents a pair of shared electrons constituting a chemical bond. We are unable to draw a single simple picture for benzene in which lines represent bonds resulting from shared electrons.

structure to another. Instead, molecules of benzene have only one electronic structure, that one structure being a difficult-to-draw hybrid of the two structures pictured in Figure 5–6. It suffices here to say that this theory accounts for the established facts concerning benzene and many other compounds and, particularly in the early days of its use, led to many new predictions that were later verified by experiment.

John Roberts, an American chemist, has devised a story to make clear what we mean by resonance. A knight of the Round Table saw a rhinoceros on one of his journeys and described it to a fellow knight as a hybrid of a unicorn and a dragon. The unicorn and dragon are imaginary creatures just as our pictures of the parent structures of benzene in Figure 5–6 are imaginary, but the rhino and the electronic structure of benzene are real. Just as the knight described the strange animal in terms that were easy for him to use, we describe the bonding in benzene and many other compounds in terms of resonance, which employs pictures that are easy to draw and use. Because, in a sense, resonance is a solution for human difficulties in describing the bonding in certain molecules, the concept should be used with care.

Experimentally determined enthalpies lead to a value of $\Delta H =$ 1323 kcal for decomposition of one mole of gaseous benzene into gaseous atoms of carbon and hydrogen. In connection with the resonance theory, it is of interest to compare this experimental quantity with the ΔH that is calculated on the basis of either of the "parent" structures shown in Figure 5–6 and bond energies from the table given earlier in this chapter.

We write the following description of the decomposition reaction of benzene:

$$(g) \rightarrow 6\,\text{C}(g) + 6\,\text{H}(g) \qquad \Delta H = +1323\,\text{kcal}$$

Six C—H bonds, three C=C and three C—C bonds are broken in this reaction scheme and we calculate that the total energy required is $(6 \times 99) + (3 \times 147) + (3 \times 83) = 1284$ kcal for each mole of benzene decomposed. Comparing this calculated value of 1284 kcal with the experimental value of $\Delta H = 1323$ kcal, we conclude that the real resonance hybrid is $1323 - 1284 = 39$ kcal per mole more stable than either of its imaginary parents. This extra stability is often called the resonance energy and was predicted by the theory.

Similar considerations for many other molecules have contributed greatly to both our understanding of bonding and to our utilization of the concept of bond energies. In "The Norwood Builder" Sherlock Holmes remarked to a visitor "You mentioned your name as if I should recognize it, but beyond the obvious facts that you are a bachelor, a solicitor, a Freemason and an asthmatic I know nothing whatever about you." The scientists who have unraveled many of the mysteries of the forces that hold atoms together in molecules and the other scientists and engineers who have combined this knowledge with energy considerations in developing products ranging from rocket fuels to Dacron shirts have had to utilize many of the detective abilities displayed by Holmes.

chapter six
man: the constant temperature energy converter

In 1774 Fedor Darapski was born in Karskod, Poland. He was drafted into the Russian Army at the age of twenty-two and soon thereafter was involved in an unsuccessful mutiny for which he was sentenced to death. In a moment of unchecked compassion, the Empress Catherine commuted his sentence to life imprisonment on a diet of two pounds of black bread and a jug of cold water per week. The generous and forgiving nature of the imperial Russian rulers ultimately caused them to reconsider Fedor's incarceration and on his ninetieth birthday he ·was released because the mutiny had never amounted to much anyway.

The first law of thermodynamics compels us to ask some questions concerning this story. Two pounds of bread per week would supply Fedor less than 400 kilocalories per day.[1] If he had been starved down to a weight of 100 pounds or less, he would have required 1200 to 1300 kilocalories per day even if he slept 12 hours and sat quietly in his cell the other 12 hours. The first law of thermodynamics, like all other laws of nature, makes no exception for man. A man must spend a certain amount of energy to maintain his body temperature and sustain his respiratory and circulatory processes. This leads us to conclude that one of the following must be true with regard to this story:

(1) Russian black bread yielded many more kilocalories per pound than any bread known today; (2) Fedor was more successful at obtaining food surreptitiously than he was at mutiny; (3)

---

[1] *Dieticians use the word* calories *when they mean* kilocalories. *We shall call a spade a spade and a strawberry shortcake a kilocalorie catastrophe.*

over the years, various storytellers have improved the tale by reducing the amount of bread that Fedor received; (4) the pound referred to was more than twice as large as our present pound.

Except for (1), any of these explanations could be true.

Man lives because he is able to utilize the chemical energy stored in the bonds between the atoms that make up his food. A living man, in many ways, is more analogous to a fuel cell (the power source used on the Gemini space capsules) than to a heat engine (to which he is frequently compared). Part of the energy passing from a high temperature source through a heat engine to a low temperature sink is used to produce work—the purpose for which the engine was built. On the other hand, a fuel cell is a constant temperature device. For instance, in one kind of fuel cell hydrogen and oxygen are combined to form water, with the resulting energy being released directly in the form of electrical power. Man is a constant temperature device that turns the energy released in him into heat and work. This released energy comes from combination of his fuel (food) with oxygen.

Galen, a Roman physician who lived around A.D. 200, speculated that an understanding of the principles of combustion would lead to an understanding of the principles of respiration. Not much progress along this line was made until the late 1770's when Antoine Lavoisier showed that air consisted largely of oxygen and nitrogen and that it was the oxygen in air that supported both combustion *and* life.[2] Lavoisier found that expired breath was

[2] *In many ways the French Revolution, in which Lavoisier was killed, was due to lack of food for the proletariat. An unsuccessful attempt was made to feed the people with gelatin made from animal waste products. There was enough gelatin to go around but people starved just the same because gelatin was not a complete protein food. Had it been a better food, history might have taken a different turn and so, no doubt, would Lavoisier's head.*

rich in carbon dioxide and also that the carbon dioxide present in the exhaled breath could not account for all the oxygen decrease in the air. The discrepancy became clear to Lavoisier when he learned of the work of the English chemist, Henry Cavendish, who showed that water was produced when hydrogen burned in the presence of oxygen. Expired breath was moist and surely food must contain hydrogen as well as carbon. It was certainly true that oxygen was consumed while water and carbon dioxide were formed when food was burned in a flame.

From the time of Hippocrates until early in the nineteenth century it was generally believed that all foods contained a single useful constituent—a universal aliment which the body extracted (nearly a ton of food per year for the average stomach), allowing the residue to go on its way. It took 2200 years for man to find out what really goes on in the utilization of food in man: the constant temperature energy converter.

The experiments of organic chemists a century ago dispatched the idea of "one universal aliment" and offered in its stead indisputable evidence that three different kinds of substances—carbohydrates, fats, and proteins—are necessary for the maintenance of life in man. These three substances yield the energy and nearly all of the material needed to sustain life and build tissue.

Carbohydrates commonly occur as starch or sugar. The chief function of carbohydrates is to supply energy. If we assimilate them and then don't utilize their chemical energy in muscular effort or in producing body heat, they are stored as fat in inconvenient and unsightly locations.

A chemical formula that typifies carbohydrates is the one for glucose; it contains six carbon atoms and the equivalent of six bound water molecules so that its formula is written $C_6H_{12}O_6$. Considering glucose as a fuel, we write the following equation for its combusion, either in a flame or in our bodies:

$$C_6H_{12}O_6 + 6\,O_2 \rightarrow 6\,CO_2 + 6\,H_2O$$

It has been found experimentally that this reaction releases 673 kilocalories per mole of glucose.[3]

A large part of the world's population is gradually making carbohydrates the mainstay of its diet. They are not doing this by choice, but by necessity, since about ten times as many calories can be obtained from an acre of corn as from the flesh of pigs fed on this same corn. Population pressures, combined with unequal distribution of the world's wealth and resources, have caused many people to increase consumption of vegetables and decrease consumption of meat and animal products. Although starches and sugars are rich in energy, they do not contain all the essentials of a good diet. Carbohydrates alone are not enough for good health or even survival.

Lipid is the Greek word for "fat." Lipids are virtually insoluble in water and have a distinctive greasy, slippery feel. Chemical investigations in France in the early nineteenth century by Michael Chevreul laid the groundwork for later proof that lipids, like carbohydrates, are composed of carbon, hydrogen, and oxygen. Although there are many lipids, a typical one is represented by the formula $C_{51}H_{98}O_6$. The chemical equation for burning this typical lipid is

$$C_{51}H_{98}O_6 + 72.5\ O_2 \rightarrow 51\ CO_2 + 49\ H_2O$$

Such a reaction releases about 7510 kilocalories per mole of lipid.

In addition to providing energy, fats perform important functions in the body. For example, fats are involved in the formation of a protective layer around many nerves. One of the consequences of semistarvation is extreme irritability, and it has been

---

[3] *In case you have forgotten, we define a mole as a counting unit of 6×10^{23} molecules having a total mass that can be calculated as the appropriate sum of atomic weights. Thus one mole of glucose is $[(6 \times 12) + (12 \times 1) + (6 \times 16)] = 180$ grams of glucose.*

suggested that this is due to the depletion of the cushioning fat around the nerves. While it is true that the body can manufacture some fat out of carbohydrates, it is quite impossible for the body to manufacture all of the necessary fats. In this connection it is interesting to note that the Arctic explorer Stefansson found life satisfactory on an all-meat diet when he ate liberally of the fat. But if he confined his eating to the lean meat, he became ill within a week. Both American Indians and Eskimos have long recognized the body's need for fat.

The third principal component of foods, protein, may be regarded as the stream of life. Genesis of life on this planet certainly was associated with or followed the formation of protein from the nonliving environment. The word itself means "of first importance" and was coined by Gerardus Johannes Mulder, a Dutch chemist, who in 1838 tried to devise a unit molecule of protein made up of a mere eighty-eight atoms. Though he failed to demonstrate that different albuminous substances (one such substance is found in the whites of eggs) could be built up of combinations of his unit molecules, his word "protein" stuck and is now universally applied to this type of matter.

The detailed structures of protein molecules are exceedingly complex—structure determinations for such substances have led to Nobel Prizes. Proteins of interest to us rarely have a molecular weight of less than 10,000 (compared to 12 for carbon and 32 for oxygen) and range upward to about 10,000,000. We can, however, simply describe chemical composition of proteins as follows: 51 to 55 per cent carbon, about 7 per cent hydrogen, 20 to 23 per cent oxygen, 15 to 19 per cent nitrogen, and 0.3 to 2.0 per cent sulfur. Some proteins also contain a little iron or phosphorus. Nature can truly do wonders with these few elements.

Plants synthesize carbohydrates (sugars and starches) from water and carbon dioxide with the aid of energy derived from sunlight. Many plants are also able to synthesize the nitrogen-containing proteins or components of proteins (amino acids) that are the basis for human and other animal life. Particularly important are the nitrogen-fixing bacteria that are associated with such plants as beans, peas, clover, and alfalfa. These bacteria living on the roots of plants are able to convert nitrogen from the air into nitrate ions, which are then assimilated by the plant and converted into protein. Bacteria are also involved in the important conversion of ammonia fertilizers and organic material in the soil to nitrate ions to be used in growth of plant proteins.

There are many amino acids that are now well characterized. An even larger number of proteins can be built up from these amino acids. One man with a liking for large numbers has computed that twenty amino acids might be combined to form at least 2,432,902,008,176,640,000 different proteins. Nature has not bothered with making all of these substances, and fortunately we can survive with just a few of them. The healthy human body can, if necessary, synthesize all of the many proteins it needs from just eight essential amino acids.

Now we take up the questions concerning the three principal dietary constituents that are relevant to the first law and energy conservation: How much energy does the body derive from the various kinds of food? How does it spend this energy?

As we saw earlier, every mole of glucose that reacts with six moles of oxygen, whether in the body or in a laboratory apparatus, releases 673 kilocalories. Combustion of a mole of typical lipid releases 7510 kilocalories. We have similar data for many other substances, including proteins. For our future discussion it is most convenient to summarize all of these data in the form of kilocalories per gram (rather than per mole), as is done in the following table.

Nowadays it seems obvious that the heat of oxidation of a food or of a component of food must be the same whether the reaction is carried out in a living body or in a combustion calorimeter. Our faith in this idea is certainly required by the first law, but it

Heats of Combustion

substance	kilocalories per gram
Hydrogen	34.2
Methane (principal component of natural gas)	13.2
Gasoline, kerosene, crude petroleum, tallow	9.5–11.5
Lipids	9.0– 9.5
Carbon	7.8
Ethyl alcohol	7.1
Proteins	4.4– 5.6*
Carbohydrates (sugars and starches)	3.6– 4.2

* These figures correspond to laboratory combustion to yield CO_2, H_2O, and oxides of nitrogen. In the body, proteins are oxidized to CO_2, H_2O, and urea. For this latter process the heat yield is less than the value indicated above. Thus proteins and carbohydrates yield (per gram) about the same energy in the body.

is comforting to know that there is also experimental confirmation. The first relevant experiments were carried out in the 1880's by Max Rubner, a German physiologist. His experiments consisted of measurements on laboratory animals in calorimeters, combined with measurements of amounts of food eaten and feces passed. After comparing the amount of food eaten with the amount that passed through, he found that each gram of digested carbohydrate yielded 4 kilocalories and each gram of lipid yielded 9 kilocalories in the body, just as in direct combustion experiments. These experiments by Rubner and later experiments by others have amply confirmed that the body produces energy by combustion and spends it by doing work or transferring heat to its environment, all in accord with the first law.

Bicycle racers spend about 8500 kilocalories per day. In terms of food requirements, that amounts to about 3½ pounds of chocolate or 7½ pounds of sirloin steak or 60 pounds of cauliflower, which explains why you never see six-day bicycle racers eating cauliflower. Lumberjacks of the old school and professional football players of the new school spend about 6000 kilocalories per day. At hard physical work, a man utilizes about 600 kilocalories per hour, while a man just sitting spends about 100 kilocalories per hour. Still lower on the energy utilization scale is the so-called basal metabolism rate, which corresponds to the rate of energy expenditure of a person who has not eaten recently and who is lying quietly (awake) in a comfortably warm room. A typical basal metabolism rate for an average adult is about 43 kilocalories per hour or about 1000 kilocalories per day. The rate of energy expenditure for a person who is sleeping is about 90 per cent of the basal metabolism rate.

A number of basal metabolism determinations have shown that nonpregnant women expend energy about 5 per cent slower than do men. Although it is contrary to current fashion, thermodynamic considerations indicate that men should wear fewer clothes than women. The basal metabolism rate on a per pound of body weight basis is about twice as fast for a one-year-old child as for an adult. There has also been noted a sharp rise in the basal metabolism rate at the onset of puberty. Neither of these last two observations should come as a surprise to normally observant parents. By age 70 the basal metabolism rate has dropped some 10 per cent below that of a middle-aged adult. Granny has good reason for turning up the thermostat and wearing an extra sweater.

Basal metabolism rates of various creatures are compared in Figure 6–1. Examination of the figure shows that a boy spends energy (on a per pound of body weight basis) faster than a man. This is not surprising, since the boy is growing and the chemical processes involved in putting new tissue in place consume energy at a very high rate. Although there are some exceptions, we conclude that large animals live longer than small animals; in a general way we can explain this longer life on the grounds that small animals live at a faster chemical pace and wear out sooner. The principal exception to this generalization linking body size and length of life is man, who lives longer than such larger creatures as elephants, horses, and gorillas. In fact, large tortoises are

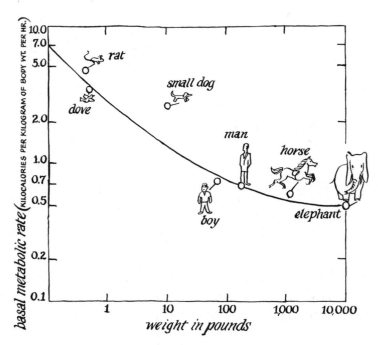

Figure 6–1. The basal metabolic rate per unit body weight as related to body weight. The larger the animal, the slower is its energy conversion on a per unit weight basis.

the only animals that commonly live longer than man, and it is well known that tortoises shun fast living.

Physicians have found the basal metabolism rate to be of considerable value in diagnosing certain kinds of human ailments, particularly those associated with glandular misbehavior. For instance, diseases of the thyroid gland may change the basal metabolism rate by as much as 25 per cent. Because of its diagnostic importance, considerable world-wide effort has been devoted to collecting data on basal metabolism rates.

The unedited transcript of a tape recording of a conversation between a physician who specializes in metabolism research and an Eskimo has recently come to our attention. Our transcription of the tape begins just after the physician and four foot lockers of equipment are unloaded from a helicopter somewhere north of the Arctic Circle.

Physician: I am here to measure your basal metabolism rate.

Eskimo: Do you wish to buy supplies?

Physician: No, thanks. I want to find out how you spend your energy and also look for hormonal differences between you and people who live in more temperate climates.

Eskimo: We are having a special on nice lean reindeer meat to make you strong and whale blubber, which is nearly all lipid, to keep you warm.

Physician: Say, I have a lot of trouble with colds in the winter. What sort of diet and treatment do you advise?

Eskimo: Do you pay cash or do you have Blue Cross?

Our translation might as well stop here, as the rest of the conversation was not much concerned with energy.

The first law of thermodynamics is certainly applicable to our bodies. If in the course of a day we eat food containing more calories (we actually mean food that will yield more calories when it is oxidized in the body) than we spend in that day, we will store the excess food, mostly as fat. An average man in good health has about 75,000 kilocalories of stored energy in his body. If he limits his activity to that of the basal state, he can survive about 75 days; the world's record for fasting is close to this period. The stored carbohydrates are used first, followed by the fat, until finally the proteins of the muscles and sinews answer the call.

People have different metabolism rates, which partly determine who will be fat, who will be lean, and who will be just right. Metabolism rates are themselves largely determined by activities of the thyroid and adrenal glands. The quantity and nature of food that is consumed also has an important bearing on whether one is called "Porky" by his acquaintances.

Nowadays most people think that they know a lot about the energy content of food because they have recently dieted or at least dreamed of doing so. Old myths, oft repeated, die hard. For instance, when a man on a diet is offered a choice between a glass of beer and a glass of orange juice, he is almost certain to choose the orange juice or at least to feel guilty about choosing the beer. But it is certainly a fact that a glass of beer and a (same size!) glass of orange juice yield the same number of calories; hence the man you have regarded as a dietary backslider may merely be one who has done his homework in thermodynamics. However, the man who nibbles Brazil nuts while he drinks beer, orange juice, or even water is clearly violating the fat man's diet. Just one-fourth pound of Brazil nuts yields 740 kilocalories while the full 12-ounce glass of beer yields "only" 165 kilocalories.

Next we lead our dieting friend to the dinner table and offer him his choice between a plate of "rich" crab meat or a "lean" steak (the usual adjectives); he is almost certain to reach for the steak without a moment's hesitation. Yet a half-pound of lean steak yields 400 kilocalories while a half-pound of rich crab meat yields only slightly more than 200 kilocalories. So don't laugh at the fat man who chooses the crab—unless he bathes it in a cheese sauce. We shall not continue this detailed discussion of the facts and fancies of energies to be obtained from various foods, but we hope we have made the point that such things are not always as most people think they are.

Before our debunking fervor departs, we make a few comments on the metabolism of alcohol. Unlike most "foods," alcohol can be taken into the bloodstream without having been digested. A small part of the alcohol that is consumed goes into the blood from the stomach while the rest passes into the small intestine and thence rapidly into the blood. The intoxicating effect of the alcohol begins only when the bloodstream carries it to the brain. If the stomach and small intestine are empty or nearly empty, alcohol makes the trip from bottle to brain very quickly.

Another interesting aspect of alcohol in the body is that it is metabolized at a nearly constant rate. For a man who weighs 160 pounds, this rate corresponds to about three-quarters of an ounce of whiskey per hour. Thus a man who consumes whiskey at this rate (one pint in 13 hours) may have digestive troubles, but he will not become more than slightly intoxicated. But if he should consume the same amount of whiskey in a much shorter time, the accumulation of alcohol in his body might be disastrous.

Since the rate of metabolism of alcohol is largely independent of other factors, the tried and not-so-true methods of "walking it off" or consuming large quantities of black coffee are largely without merit. The stimulating coffee counteracts some of the depressant action of alcohol on the brain and therefore helps keep a drunk awake—but asleep or awake, he is still drunk.

The metabolism of alcohol by way of acetaldehyde (more toxic than alcohol) and acetic acid to carbon dioxide and water is a simple process compared to the metabolism of the usual complicated foods. In general, the body neither stores nor directly utilizes the carbohydrates, lipids, and proteins it receives as food. Instead, through a series of metabolic processes, it converts the large and complex molecules it receives into relatively simple molecules. These processes are called *catabolism* (from the Greek word meaning "to throw downward"). Thus digestion turns unabsorbable food into absorbable structural units. More specifically, the digestion process results in conversion of carbohydrates to glucose and similar substances, while digestion of lipids yields glycerol (commonly called glycerin) and various fatty acids which are chemical brothers of the acetic acid that is the active component of vinegar.

After catabolism of carbohydrates and lipids has proceeded to glucose, glycerol, and fatty acids, further catabolism of these substances occurs. This further catabolism is the oxidation of these substances by oxygen that is taken in through the lungs and ultimately yields carbon dioxide and water. These catabolic oxidations, which are chemically equivalent to the burning reactions that can take place in a calorimeter or on a bonfire, are the principal sources of the energy required to keep the human machine running.

The proteins that are consumed in meat, cheese, and certain vegetables are first catabolized to the amino acids, which may be regarded as the building blocks of the original proteins. Some of the resulting amino acids are further catabolized to water, carbon dioxide, and urea. These reactions yield useful energy in the body, but for energy production are generally less important than the reactions discussed in the preceding paragraph.

Although the body does not directly store the lipids and proteins it receives as food, we know by observation that the body does contain both protein and lipid material. These complex lipids and proteins are formed in the body by processes that are the reverse of the catabolic processes we have been discussing. This building of complex molecules from simpler ones is called *anabolism* (from the Greek word meaning "to throw upward"). Specifically, the anabolic processes combine glycerol and fatty acids to form lipids and combine amino acids to form proteins. These proteins differ from those that were consumed—not so much in terms of components but rather in terms of how the components are linked together.

These building or anabolic processes require energy, which is made available by the catabolic processes described earlier. The relation between these processes is shown graphically in Figure 6–2. Without recourse to scientific terminology, Shakespeare summarized these related processes with the following words in *As You Like It:*

> And so from hour to hour we ripe and ripe,
> And then from hour to hour, we rot and rot;
> And thereby hangs a tale.

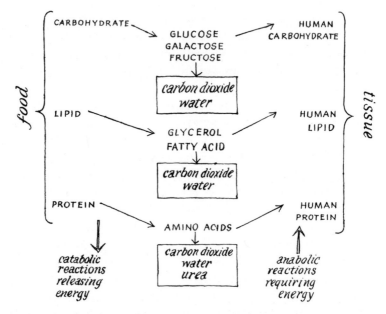

Figure 6–2. An oversimplified scheme of metabolism in the human body. Reactions with arrows pointing down release energy (catabolism); reactions with arrows pointing up require energy (anabolism).

The tale that we are concerned with is what the first law of thermodynamics says about these catabolic and anabolic processes. Since the first law can be regarded as a prescription or set of directions for energy accounting, it behooves us to set up an outline of those processes that yield energy in the body and those processes that are accompanied by consumption of energy. As we have already written, catabolic processes are exothermic: they yield the energy that is required for anabolic processes. These tissue-building processes take place in all of us, but occur to a greater extent in a growing boy than in a sedentary adult—unless the adult is rapidly becoming obese. In addition to the energy-consuming anabolic processes, our bodies spend their energy income from catabolic processes by radiating heat to the surroundings, by playing football, or by reading scientific treatises, etc. If we loosely describe the energy expended in all these latter ways as "work energy," we can write the following equation:

catabolic energy to spend = anabolic energy spent
$$+ \text{"work energy" spent}$$

Since the production of catabolic energy depends on the fuel that is available, we see why growing boys seem like bottomless pits at mealtime.

People require energy to live; the animals that surround man require energy to live; and the plants that surround and support man and other animals require energy to live and to grow. Where does all this energy come from, and how much total energy income does our world have?

Fortunately, our earth receives a tremendous amount of energy from that wondrous star that is just the right distance from us— the sun. Only a tiny fraction of the sun's total output of energy reaches the earth, but even that tiny fraction is a huge amount of energy—about 4×10^{13} kilocalories per second, according to Farrington Daniels, a chemist who has devoted considerable study to the utilization of solar energy. This is the amount of energy that can be obtained by combustion of 6,000,000 *tons* of coal per second! We can touch on only part of the extensive story of utilization of some of this energy by living organisms.

In 1779 Jan Ingenhousz, a Dutch physician, published a book in which he clearly pointed out that a balanced relationship exists between plant and animal life on earth. Plants spend energy that they have absorbed in the form of sunlight to utilize carbon dioxide and water (also other substances in lesser amounts) to form their own structures, that is, leaves, trunks, etc. This process of building from carbon dioxide and water with light as the energy source is now called *photosynthesis*, which may be traced back to Greek words meaning "put together by light." Ingenhousz also noted that animals live by combining plant material with oxygen to produce carbon dioxide, water, and the energy they require for their continued existence.

If we describe a typical carbohydrate by the average formula $C_6H_{12}O_6$, we can write the photosynthesis reaction as

$$6\,CO_2 + 6\,H_2O + \text{energy (from light)} \rightarrow C_6H_{12}O_6 + 6\,O_2$$

We write the metabolic reaction that occurs when an animal has eaten the plant as the reverse of the photosynthesis reaction above, that is:

$$C_6H_{12}O_6 + 6\,O_2 \rightarrow 6\,CO_2 + 6\,H_2O + \text{energy}$$

Thus carbon, hydrogen, and oxygen shuttle back and forth between plants and animals in a way that is sometimes called "the carbon cycle." And it is the energy from the sun that literally keeps us going, although plants are necessary intermediates and certain animals are unessential but tasty intermediates.

Further consideration of the energy transformations involved in the round robin carbon cycle will permit us to draw some interesting conclusions about the maximum amount of life that the earth can support. To draw these conclusions, it is necessary once again to apply the principle of conservation of energy—the first law of thermodynamics.

Only about 10 per cent of the energy derived from the food he consumes can be used by man for operating the processes that build and replace tissue. The other 90 per cent of available energy is devoted to maintaining body temperature, to hustling food for the next meal, and to a variety of other activities. Furthermore, and inevitably, some of the energy derived from consumed food is wasted as required by another law of thermodynamics—the second.

Now let us take as a rough sort of generalization that 10 pounds of digestible food can yield at most only 1 pound of tissue. If tigers live on gazelles and gazelles feed on grass, there must be at least 10 pounds of grass for every pound of gazelle and at least 100 pounds of grass for every pound of tiger. This is a simple example of a food chain or pyramid, as illustrated in Figure 6–3. The pyramid is necessarily rather squat, since the example of grass → gazelle → tiger shows that there can never be very many links in the chain or steps in the pyramid. Carnivores that live on smaller herbivores are clearly an inefficient form of life.

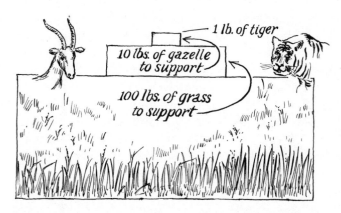

Figure 6–3. A food chain showing the amount of food needed to support one pound of tiger. The ultimate source of energy for every link in the chain is, of course, the sun.

It has long been recognized that a species may increase its total mass on earth by eliminating one or more links in the food chain. If tigers could or would live directly on grass, their food supply would increase at least tenfold and there could be ten times more tigers. It is thus no accident that the largest land animals extant today are herbivores such as the elephant, hippopotamus, and rhinoceros. Next we consider how all this affects man and his numbers on earth.

The fusion of hydrogen to form helium in the sun yields about

8×10^{21} kilocalories per second. This huge yield of energy is derived from the loss of mass that occurs on fusion and can be related to mass by Einstein's famous equation, $E = mc^2$, which can be written as $\Delta E = (\Delta m)c^2$ for the case of conversion of mass to energy. Some arithmetic with this equation will show that the sun loses about 4,200,000 tons per second, which should give you something new to worry about. But the important figure for us to consider is the 4×10^{13} kilocalories per second that reach the earth from the sun. How much of this energy can be utilized directly or indirectly for the maintenance of man on earth?

First let us consider the fate of the radiant energy that reaches the earth from the sun. About half of this energy is reflected into space. Isaac Asimov has studied the problem of what happens to the remaining energy and estimates that about 3 per cent falls on green plants and that about two-thirds of this amount is actually absorbed. Then only about two-thirds of the absorbed energy is effectively used in the production of carbohydrate material. The following multiplication indicates how much energy may be used in carbohydrate production:

$$4 \times 10^{13} \frac{\text{kcal}}{\text{sec}} \times \tfrac{1}{2} \times \tfrac{3}{100} \times \tfrac{2}{3} \times \tfrac{2}{3} = 3 \times 10^{11} \frac{\text{kcal}}{\text{sec}}$$

On the basis of our previous statement that animals can use only about 10 per cent of the energy they develop from catabolism of carbohydrates for building new tissue, we see that no more than about 3×10^{10} kilocalories per second can be used to support animal life.

The available energy for support of animal life corresponds to about 2.5×10^{15} kilocalories per day. On the basis of 2000 kilocalories per day for each person, we calculate that the maximum human population on the earth is about 1×10^{12} people—1000 billion. The present population is about 3 billion or 3×10^9. Thus the maximum population is some 300 times the present population of the world. In considering this possible population, it is important to keep in mind that we have assumed that people are the only plant-eating animals and that we have not distinguished between land and ocean.

We can arrive at a more realistic maximum population by allowing for the fact that some nonhuman animal life on the land is inevitable, with consequent inefficient use of carbohydrate material. Further, there will certainly be considerable animal life in the oceans to diminish further the efficiency with which carbohydrates are used. Considerations of this sort suggest that the maximum population that can be supported with energy that the earth receives from the sun is about 150 billion people—50 times the present population of the world.

All of the figures given in the preceding paragraphs are based on limitations imposed solely by the amounts of available energy. Since man cannot live on carbohydrate alone, we should also consider the availability of protein, vitamins, and even the total amount of carbon in the world that can be used for plant and people growth. Nowadays we get most of our protein directly or indirectly from animals, which is a luxury that cannot be afforded when the population of the world increases severalfold. But it does appear that it is possible to produce enough protein on the earth to keep some 30 to 40 times the present population of the world alive—just barely.

Perhaps some individual men can live on bread alone, but society certainly requires more than carbohydrates, vegetable oils, and synthetic proteins. Aside from a desire for comfort and privacy, both clothing and shelter are absolutely necessary in many parts of the world. Further, it will require both energy and material to build and operate the machinery that will be used to harvest and distribute the carbohydrates and other foods. There will also be problems associated with shortages of fossil fuels, inadequate supplies of potable water for both people and plants, sewage disposal, and on and on. Invoking the hoped-for availability of nearly unlimited energy derived from nuclear reactors is necessary, but by no means solves all of the problems associated with a world population much greater than the present 3 billion.

All of these considerations show that a practical maximum possible population on the earth cannot actually be as large as any of the figures given in the preceding paragraphs. Since this practical maximum depends as much on man's efficiency in organizing his collective affairs and the standard of living he is willing to tolerate as on energy considerations, the best we can do is make a rough estimate that this practical maximum is from five to ten times the present population. It takes very little scientific knowledge or even imagination to realize that life under the conditions we would necessarily have with a population only five times the present 3 billion would be far from pleasant.

It is quite clear that thermodynamics and shortages of both space and material will cause the population of the world to stop growing at some point. It is also quite clear that it is to the advantage of all humans to stop this growth long before the population reaches its ultimate maximum. War, starvation, or birth control can stabilize or even decrease the population of the world. Take your choice.

Most of this chapter has been devoted to considerations of too little food, either individually for Fedor Darapski or collectively for the population of the world. Now we briefly consider the opposite problem of too much food, again in terms of the first law.

After age thirty, the metabolic rate drops, but the appetite for food is often undiminished. The first law tells us what is commonly known from experience: if you take in more food than you consume as fuel, you store the unused food as fat. This is by no means a new problem.

In the 1830's a New Englander writing in a journal of that day argued that even the tables of that thrifty region were too heavy for the good of the populace:

Long has my soul been grieved at the thought of the incalcu-
lable quantity of fish, fowl and flesh which is devoured daily
by my countrymen. It may be stated that everyone in the
United States eats one-fourth more than is good for them.
Those not doing hard work indulge in abominable excesses.
. . . While men lived on acorns and water from a stream
there was no temptation to eat too much, but when roast meat
and strong waters came into use, they brought crime, violence
and war in train.

The author of these stirring lines proposed a solution in the form
of a Society for the Suppression of Eating. The duties and obli-
gations of members of the Society were simple enough:

(1) Obtain from the Massachusetts Medical Society a statement
of the quantity of food required for good health.
(2) Forego dinner once a week.
(3) Eat only once per day.
(4) Never eat after eight at night.

When last heard from, the Society was not flourishing.

chapter seven
time's arrow

Rivers could flow uphill if the river beds in which they flow were to cool slightly, giving up thermal energy to the river water and thus conserving the energy of the universe. But they don't.

The water in the river might dissociate spontaneously into hydrogen and oxygen at the expense of the thermal energy of the surroundings. But it doesn't.

The air above the river might spontaneously liquefy, liberating thermal energy to its surroundings; or it might separate, spontaneously, into pure oxygen and nitrogen. But it doesn't.

Furthermore, an old man sitting on the river bank watching the river flow by might grow young—his wrinkles might disappear, his hair might grow thick and black, and his muscles might become taut and resilient. But, alas, none of these things happen.

In each case the first law of thermodynamics could be satisfied without difficulty. Each event hypothesized above is the reverse of an actual happening. Rivers flow downhill, hydrogen and oxygen form water (sometimes explosively) and liberate thermal energy to the surroundings, liquid air absorbs thermal energy from its surroundings (unless they are very cold) and evaporates. Man inevitably grows old, and in the process he frequently acquires wrinkles, gray hair, and a flabby paunch. In the next three chapters we tell why the reverse of these events doesn't take place. In each case the answer comes down to the statement that the second law of thermodynamics says that while each of the events described is conceivable, each is so highly unlikely that it is practically impossible.

Nowadays people have no difficulty in accepting the first law of thermodynamics, which often seems to be a pretty obvious bit of common sense. But the second law is different. It sometimes seems to be a "True, but so what?" law, and at other times seems to run contrary to "common sense." We shall see, however, that this law leads us into many strange and wondrous areas where the first law alone is of little interest or importance.

Because the second law of thermodynamics may be stated in so many different forms, it may be construed by many to be an ill-defined law and, therefore, not a *really* important law of nature. This is not so. It is just because it is statable in so many forms that it has become a thread that weaves its way through all aspects of science and life. A. S. Eddington, a noted British astronomer, stated it succinctly in the Gifford Lectures of 1927 when he said:

> The law that entropy always increases—the second law of thermodynamics—holds, I think, the supreme position among the laws of Nature. If someone points out to you that your pet theory of the universe is in disagreement with Maxwell's equations—then so much the worse for Maxwell's equations. If it is found to be contradicted by observation—well, these experimentalists do bungle things sometimes. But if your theory is found to be against the second law of thermodynamics, I can give you no hope; there is nothing for it but to collapse in deepest humiliation.

Scientists have found it both necessary and convenient when discussing heat to express themselves quantitatively. To do so adequately, at least two numbers must be used: one to measure the quantity of energy, the other to measure the quantity of disorder. The calorie has proved suitable for measuring the quantity of energy. The quantity of disorder is measured in terms of the *entropy*.[1]

[1] *Clausius gave us this name after observing that the ratio of heat to temperature had special properties. He first called it* Verwandlungsinhalt *(transformation-content) because it measured the transformability of heat. Later he called it entropy, which comes*

The idea of entropy is bound inextricably with all our theoretical ideas about heat and certain other phenomena, including information. One way of defining entropy is in terms of the number of states that are possible in a system in a given situation. The disorder arises because we do not know which state the system is in. Disorder [2] is then essentially the same thing as ignorance, which is how entropy is related to information theory. In unsophisticated terms, entropy is a measure of the number of independent degrees of freedom that a system has. A high entropy system is free to be in many different states. We might make this point a little clearer by examining the value of entropy per mole for some different substances at room temperature and atmospheric pressure.

---

from two Greek stems meaning "turning into." We believe that considering both words, on balance, it was a fortunate change. Stephen Leacock commented on this quantity: "All physicists sooner or later say, 'Let us call it entropy,' just as a man says, when you get to know him, 'Call me Charlie.'"

[2] *Disorder is a tricky fellow to pin down. Everyone knows what it means to shuffle a pack of cards and would be willing to claim that a deck had been well shuffled after observing the shuffling and resulting hands dealt by a good (and honest) card player. Is it possible to describe the shuffle as good when only the shuffling operation is specified or is it necessary to know the results of a shuffle before one can say it is good? G. N. Lewis, an American chemist, has pointed out correctly that it would be possible to formulate the rules of some card game so that any arrangement of the cards whatever would be a "regular" arrangement from the point of view of that game. (Is there a poker player alive who has not played at least one game of 5-card draw with twos, threes, fives, and one-eyed jacks wild?) Disorder is not an absolute concept; rather it is relative and has meaning only in context.*

Substance	Entropy
	[cal/(°K-mole)]
Diamond	0.6
Platinum	10.0
Lead	15.5
Water (liquid)	16.7
Laughing gas	62.6

Examination of this table reveals that entropy is closely related to hardness. In fact, hard, abrasive materials such as diamond, garnet, topaz, and silicon carbide in which individual atoms are bound together in three-dimensional lattices by chemical bonds that severely limit thermal motion of the atoms have small entropies. It is also apparent that soft substances such as gases contain large amounts of thermal disorder (their molecules are shooting about in every direction with a wide variety of speeds) at room temperature and thus have large entropies.

Since entropy is a measure of the molecular randomness in a system, we expect that there will be an increase in entropy associated with melting a solid (little randomness) to a liquid (more randomness) or evaporating a liquid to a gas (most randomness). The increase in entropy for melting ice is 5.3 cal/(°K-mole) and for boiling water is 25.7 cal/(°K-mole).

Entropy has another useful function in that it can provide a rigorous definition of temperature. Temperature (T) may be defined as the ratio of the change in energy of a system (ΔE) to its change in entropy (ΔS) for a constant volume (zero work) process:

$$T = \frac{\text{increase in energy}}{\text{increase in entropy}} = \frac{\Delta E}{\Delta S}$$

This way of looking at the absolute temperature says it is the quantity of energy that must be added to a system to alter its entropy one unit. For example, if we have to add 375 calories of thermal energy to a system to alter its entropy by one entropy unit (1 cal/°K), then the temperature of the system is 375 calories per entropy unit; thus the temperature of the system is 375°K as shown by:

$$T = \frac{\Delta E}{\Delta S} = \frac{375 \text{ cal}}{1 \text{ cal/°K}} = 375°K$$

The increase in entropy of a substance when thermal energy is added to it is proportional to the amount of thermal energy added. The entropy of a cold substance is altered more by the addition of one calorie of thermal energy than is the entropy of a hot substance. This definition of temperature has the virtue of being precise even though it may not convey much information in a qualitative sense about temperature. It is also a definition of temperature that does not depend on the particular properties of the thermometers used to measure it. A mercury thermometer, of course, depends on the properties of mercury and the glass that make up the thermometer. Unfortunately, we do not have convenient "entropy meters" which would allow us to make everyday use of this definition of temperature.

Now that we have a little background in the subjects of order, disorder, entropy, and the like we can move on to the second law of thermodynamics.

On the left-hand side of Figure 7–1 we see a book floating a few feet above the floor; on the right the book has fallen to the floor where its potential energy has been converted to heat (and perhaps a little sound energy). The lengths of the arrows in the drawing represent the magnitude of the random thermal motion of the molecules in the floor. This random thermal motion is greater in State 2 than in State 1. State 2 is a state of greater microscopic disorder and is intrinsically much more probable than State 1. Keep in mind that substances at higher temperatures have greater thermal energy, which causes their molecules to be in a more disordered state. Now let us examine the reverse process—the book going from State 2 to State 1. Our experience tells us that the floor does not spontaneously give up thermal energy (floor gets cooler) to the book, thus raising the book a few feet above the floor. That is to say, microscopic disorder or entropy

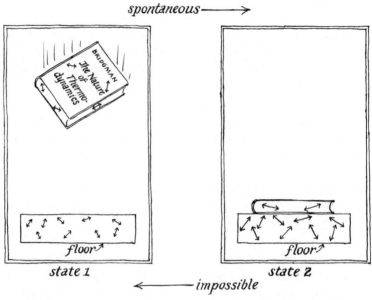

Figure 7-1. The spontaneous process (book falls to floor) is one in which potential energy is converted to random thermal energy, thus increasing the total entropy. The impossible process (book flying) would convert random thermal energy into potential energy and might ultimately lead to a something-for-nothing machine.

does not spontaneously decrease. Henry A. Bent, a chemist at the University of Minnesota, has made calculations which show that it is *more likely* for a tribe of wild monkeys, punching randomly on a set of typewriters, to turn out Shakespeare's complete works fifteen quadrillion times in succession without error than is the conversion at room temperature of one calorie of thermal energy to work.[3]

Consider a piece of ice floating in a glass of water resting on a table, the whole arrangement (except for the ice) being at room temperature. The ice melts and in so doing it cools the water in the glass and the portion of the table under the glass. As this process is carried out, the ice changes from the ordered solid state to the disordered liquid state. The entropy increase of the ice is greater than the entropy decrease of the water in the glass and the table, which are both cooled by the melting of the ice.

We have not observed (and do not ever expect to observe) the reverse of this process whereby a portion of the water and the table spontaneously absorb energy from another portion of the water and produce a piece of ice in the glass. Once again we observe that microscopic disorder (entropy) does not spontaneously decrease.

We can go through a similar argument for a closed can (called a bomb by chemists) containing one mole of hydrogen gas and one-half mole of oxygen gas at room temperature. If a slight activation energy (a match or an electric arc) is supplied to this mixture, it will release a great deal of energy (68 kilocalories) to its surroundings and produce one mole of liquid water. We have never observed the reverse reaction in which the surroundings spontaneously give up 68 kilocalories of energy and dissociate water into hydrogen and oxygen. *Microscopic disorder (entropy) of a system and its surroundings (all of the relevant universe) does not spontaneously decrease.*

[3] *Thermodynamicists may be divided into two camps, depending upon where they were educated and their current socioeconomic status. The first group always makes probabilistic calculations and statements of the above nature about monkeys typing the complete works of Shakespeare; the second group always has the monkeys type all the books in the British Museum.*

We call this sentence a statement of the second law of thermo-dynamics. And we know that it is correct.[4]

The flow of thermal energy from a hot object is a process that requires no assistance from anyone. Take the roast out of the oven and, while the guests leisurely seat themselves around the table, the roast inevitably cools. If our previous statement of the second

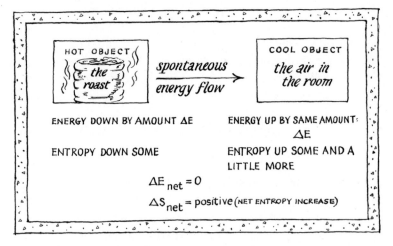

Figure 7–2. The spontaneous energy flow must occur so that there is a net increase in entropy for the entire system of interest.

law is applicable, then the entropy of the universe (the roast plus the air in the dining room) is greater after the cooling process takes place than it was before. This is true despite the fact that the hot object decreases its entropy, because the cold surround-ings are gaining thermal energy and thus entropy at the same time. The loss of entropy of the roast is more than made up for by the gain in entropy of the air in the room. We indicate this in a qualitative way in Figure 7–2.

[4] *Richard Bellman said, "What I tell you three times is true."*

We now have a test to use to determine which way a process will proceed. For example, the test says that thermal energy will flow [5] to produce a net increase in entropy.

Figure 7–3. Energy and entropy calculations for a thermal interchange between two objects. We know by experience that energy spontaneously flows from hot objects to cold objects. If energy (heat) ever flowed spontaneously from cold to hot objects (very similar to water flowing uphill), we could build a useful perpetual motion machine of the second kind.

Now consider the specific process pictured in Figure 7–3. We have a hot object at 500°K that undergoes an energy transfer of 1000 calories of thermal energy to a cooler object at 400°K. Both objects are so large that losing or gaining 1000 calories does not appreciably change their temperatures. It is shown in the calculations with Figure 7–3 that the thermal energy passes from the hot object to the cold object, since if it were to go the other way it would result in an entropy decrease. We are thus led to another statement of the second law of thermodynamics:

[5] *The second law, like the other laws of thermodynamics, is silent about the rate of natural processes. It says thermal energy will flow from the hot to the cold reservoir; a bouncing ball will come to rest, eventually. But how long is eventually? Seconds or eons? The second law doesn't say. Its NO is emphatic; its YES is only permissive.*

> No process is possible whose sole effect is the removal of heat
> from a reservoir at one temperature and the absorption of an
> equal quantity of heat by a reservoir at a higher temperature.

This is known as the Clausius statement of the second law and is
named after Rudolf Clausius, one of the founders of classical
thermodynamics.

A machine that can produce useful mechanical work from the
natural flow of thermal energy from high temperatures to lower
temperatures is called a *heat engine*. Since the second law was
originally stated in terms of heat engines, we shall formulate such
a statement that is equivalent to our previous statements.

Consider our previous calculations on thermal energy flow
shown in Figure 7–3. In order to prevent the entropy of the universe from decreasing, we are only required to have 800 calories
go to the reservoir at 400°K. This may be calculated as follows:
For reservoir 1:

$$\Delta S_1 = \frac{\Delta E_1}{T_1} = \frac{-1000 \text{ calories}}{500°\text{K}} = -2 \frac{\text{calories}}{°\text{K}}$$

For reservoir 2 the entropy must increase the same amount:

$$\Delta S_2 = \frac{\Delta E_2}{T_2} = \frac{+800 \text{ calories}}{400°\text{K}} = +2 \frac{\text{calories}}{°\text{K}}$$

We are therefore free to dispose of the remainder of the energy
in any way we choose, including the performance of useful work.
So we rearrange our thermal reservoirs and insert a heat engine
between them, as shown in Figure 7–4. An energy and entropy
balance can now be carried out on these three bodies which are
experiencing the following effects: (1) The hot object at 500°K
loses 1000 calories and has its entropy decreased by 2 cal/°K.
(2) The cooler object at 400°K receives 800 calories of thermal
energy and has its entropy increased by 2 cal/°K. (3) The engine
located between them converts the surplus 200 calories to mechanical work and raises the weight the appropriate distance.

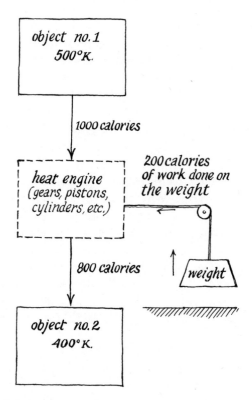

Figure 7–4. A heat engine employs a temperature difference to do work.

Summarizing:

	change in energy (cal)	change in entropy (cal/°K)
500-degree thermal reservoir	−1000	−2
400-degree thermal reservoir	+ 800	+2
Weight	+ 200	0
Net for all three objects	0	0

From the above table we see that energy is certainly conserved as that column adds to zero. We also note that the entropy of the universe does not decrease, so the second law is not violated. We might add that heat engines that operate without producing entropy are called reversible engines; the particular engine of this type of most interest to us is called a Carnot engine. It is named after Sadi Carnot, a French scientist about whom we will say more a little later. Heat engines that produce entropy increases are called irreversible or real engines. According to the second law, there can be no heat engines that produce net entropy decreases.

Examination of the table reveals that perhaps we have punished ourselves unnecessarily. Why throw away 800 calories to the cooler reservoir; why not just 600 calories or even better yet zero calories to the cooler reservoir? That would leave more energy for the engine to use in raising the weight. Unfortunately, if we transfer (waste) one calorie less than 800 to the cold reservoir, its entropy would not increase by $+2$ cal/°K and the net change in entropy for the system would be negative. For example, if we transfer only 600 calories to the cold reservoir

$$\Delta S_2 = \Delta E_2/T_2 = +600/400 = +1.5 \text{ cal}/°\text{K};$$

but

$$\Delta S_{\text{net}} = \Delta S_1 + \Delta S_2 = -2 + 1.5 = -0.5 \text{ cal}/°\text{K}.$$

We have already stated as one form of the second law of thermodynamics that entropy cannot spontaneously decrease in a system isolated from its surroundings. Thus it is seen to be impossible to transfer just 600 calories; in fact, we must transfer 800 calories *or more*. We may now generalize our observations into another statement of the second law:

It is impossible to construct a heat engine that can operate more efficiently than a Carnot engine operating between the same temperatures.

Let us carry out a simple series of thought experiments that will illuminate another aspect of the second law of thermodynamics. Consider a box divided into two sections by a partition with a small hole in it. Assume that we have available to us equipment that will allow us to introduce identical molecules one at a time into the box; these molecules are free to go to either side of the box. First we place just one molecule in the box. The number of possible states for the molecule in the box is two—that is, the molecule is either in the left or in the right portion of the box:

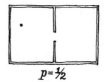 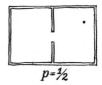

$p=\frac{1}{2}$ $p=\frac{1}{2}$

The probability that the molecule is in one side or the other is one-half; both states are equally likely to occur. The probabilities for both states must add up to one, since it is a certainty that the molecule is in the box somewhere.

We now consider the case of two molecules in the box. There are four possible states: two molecules on the left, two molecules on the right, and two states with a molecule on each side. We note that in this last case we can get a molecule on each side two different ways because we can always interchange the left molecule with the right and the right with the left (since they are identical). Thus,

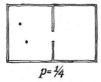 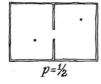 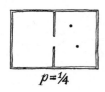

$p=\frac{1}{4}$ $p=\frac{1}{2}$ $p=\frac{1}{4}$

We observe that the center arrangement is the most likely to occur because it has a probability twice that of the other arrangements.

Once again we note that the probabilities add to unity since it is a certainty that the molecules will take up one of these arangements.

The probability that n events will occur simultaneously is simply the product of the probability of the individual events occurring.[6] Since the probability that one molecule will be on a given side is $\frac{1}{2}$, the probability that all n molecules in a system will simultaneously be on one side is $(\frac{1}{2})^n$. Thus for a system of four molecules the probability of all four being on one side is $\frac{1}{2} \times \frac{1}{2} \times \frac{1}{2} \times \frac{1}{2} = \frac{1}{16}$. Probabilities of other arrangements are as follows:

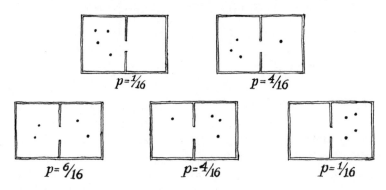

The probability of forming the second state is $\frac{4}{16}$ since there are four different ways to form each of these states. Similarly, the probability of forming the middle state is $\frac{6}{16}$.

[6] *Simple probability calculations can also be quite revealing in the examination of certain occupations. Consider the football parlay card where the point spreads are chosen by an expert. On such cards the probability of picking a single winner is about one-half. Then the probability of choosing three winners out of three picks is $(\frac{1}{2})^3 = \frac{1}{8}$, and the probability of choosing ten winners out of ten picks is $(\frac{1}{2})^{10} = \frac{1}{1024}$. Who gets rich when parlay cards offer odds of four to one for picking three winners out of three attempts and one hundred to one for picking ten winners out of ten attempts?*

We summarize some conclusions that can be reached from considerations of these and similar illustrations for larger numbers of molecules as follows: (1) As the number of molecules involved increases, the probability that all will be simultaneously in one side of the box becomes very small (with n equal only to ten the probability becomes less than one in a thousand); (2) the molecules are most likely to be distributed evenly between the two sides of the box. Here it is important to recognize that the relatively great probability of the evenly divided distribution as compared to the distribution with all molecules on one side arises from the large number of ways in which an even distribution can be obtained as compared to the single way in which one can obtain a distribution with all molecules on one side. We associate a large number of ways in which a given distribution can be obtained with randomness or molecular disorder and thence high entropy. Order and low entropy are associated with states that can be achieved in only a small number of ways.

We conclude that if we introduce a number of molecules into one side of the box and uncover the small hole between the two parts, it is highly unlikely that the molecules will stay on that side. They will arrange themselves from a state of low probability (low entropy) to the state of maximum probability (high entropy)—that is, they will soon distribute themselves as uniformly as possible throughout the box. Two American chemists, Gilbert N. Lewis and M. Randall, generalized this observation for all natural physical phenomena by writing:

> Every system which is left to itself will, on the average, change toward a condition of maximum probability.[7]

This last statement is a general statement of the second law of thermodynamics and is seen to be equivalent to our earlier state-

---

[7] *Sometimes paraphrased as: If you think things are mixed up now, just wait.*

ment about the impossibility of microscopic disorder decreasing spontaneously. Man creates local and temporary islands of decreasing entropy in a world in which the entropy as a whole certainly increases, and it is the existence of these islands that enables some of us to assert the existence of progress.

The reader must not be discouraged if his understanding of the second law and entropy do not appear crystal-clear at this point. Many scientists and engineers regard entropy as a convenient mathematical function—simply a ratio of heat to temperature, nothing more and nothing less. They regard all attempts to give it a physical meaning as futile. As Morton Mott-Smith has pointed out, velocity could also be regarded as merely a useful mathematical function, the ratio of distance to time. However, because of our direct experience with motion, velocity means more to us than a mere ratio. But we can have no direct experience with entropy; we cannot feel it like temperature or see its effects like heat. Our knowledge of it is necessarily roundabout and our conception will always be a little vague. Boltzmann, who discovered the mathematical relation between entropy and probability, once said, "How awkward is the human mind in divining the nature of things, when forsaken by the analogy of what we see and touch directly."

All other variables with which science is concerned can be increased or decreased—but entropy and time always increase. Entropy can only be decreased temporarily and then only in a localized region at the expense of a greater increase elsewhere. It is a one-way variable that marks the universe as older today than it was yesterday. Entropy, as Arthur Eddington expressed it, is "Time's Arrow."

The beginning of the nineteenth century was a time of change—Europe was entering a new era, the age of steam power and iron. It was during this period that some of the most creative minds of science came forth and rendered works of extreme importance.

In 1824 a small book by Sadi Carnot, entitled *Reflections on the Motive Power of Fire* (*Réflexions sur la puissance motrice du feu et sur les machines*), was published in Paris. It was in this slender volume that the roots of the second law of thermodynamics were first exposed to the light of day.

In his book Carnot made several distinct contributions to the science of heat. They included:

(1) The introduction of the concept of the cycle. A series of processes can bring a system back to its initial condition. For example, air or steam in a cylinder can be compressed, heated, expanded, and cooled and brought back to exactly the same state it was in before it was compressed.

(2) The second idea concerned the concept of reversibility. A reversible process is one that ideally can be carried out without friction or dissipation. In a reversible process the entropy change that occurs in the forward part of the process is exactly offset by an equal but opposite entropy change that occurs in the backward part of the process.

(3) Lastly, Carnot stated a new principle concerning the maximum work obtainable from a heat engine. This principle is the first statement of the second law of thermodynamics. One of the forms in which he stated it was as follows:

> The motive power of heat is independent of the agents employed to realize it; its quantity is fixed solely by the temperature of the bodies between which is effected, finally, the transfer of caloric.

It is ironic that Carnot discovered the second law before the first had been established. The consequences of this situation had considerable impact on the development of thermodynamics. For a while it meant that Joule could not accept Carnot's principle and Kelvin could not accept Joule's principle. The unpublished notes left by Carnot indicate that this confusion might have been resolved sooner had it not been for his death in 1832 at age thirty-six.

Carnot explained the production of work in his cyclic engine by saying it was analogous to a waterwheel; he explained (incorrectly) that a certain quantity of heat flowed into his engine at a high temperature and the same quantity flowed out at a low temperature. This explanation was consistent with the caloric theory, which required that the net heat interaction of the cycle be zero. Since Carnot had no other theory of heat to use, he accepted and used this misconception.

In 1848, Kelvin, who knew and respected the works of both Joule and Carnot, could not reconcile Carnot's hydraulic analogy with Joule's concept of the convertibility of heat and work. Two years later Clausius picked out what was relevant from Carnot and Joule's work. After reviewing the questions Kelvin posed, he suggested that the answer lay in the kinetic or motion theory of heat. He pointed out that the first law (Mayer, Joule, and Helmholtz) could be entirely reconciled with Carnot's theory merely by rejecting Carnot's subsidiary statement that caloric is conserved.

Clausius' work crystallized the whole scheme for Kelvin. Within a year he wrote a 150-page paper in the *Transactions of the Royal Society* in which he attributed the first law to Joule and the second to Carnot and Clausius.[8] In 1852 Joule and Kelvin proposed the thermodynamic temperature scale which bears the latter's

[8] *In 1865 Clausius succinctly summarized in two lines the first two laws of thermodynamics:*
     Die Energie der Welt ist constant.
     Die Entropie der Welt strebt einem Maximum zu.
It is always a sign of high scholarship to quote authors in the language in which they wrote. Besides, it will keep the reader who is not knowledgeable in the language reading on to see if the quoting authors translate the statement later in the book.

name. Then Clausius defined entropy as the property that charac-terizes the second law in the same way that energy characterizes the first law. Thus, before 1860, the foundations of classical thermodynamics were established.

Most of the huge structure of modern thermodynamics, which extends from technological applications to philosophy and poetry, is built on the solid foundation of the first and second laws. In *Life on the Mississippi,* Mark Twain wrote: "There is something fascinating about science, one gets such wholesale returns of conjectures out of such a trifling investment of fact." If we change "conjectures" to "certainty," Twain's facetious statement truly describes the achievements based on the pioneering work of Carnot, Mayer, Joule, Helmholtz, Clausius, and Kelvin.

chapter eight
equilibrium: the arrow's target

We all know by experience and "common sense" that there is a natural direction for a great variety of processes: rocks roll downhill, middle-aged men grow old, cold water freezes, and hot water boils away. The first law of thermodynamics gives us useful rules for keeping energy accounts for these processes; the second law points these processes in the natural direction.

But Time's Arrow, which is guided by the second law, is trickier than any arrow ever used by a sensible buffalo hunter since this Arrow can turn around and point the other way. For instance, we all agree that it is natural for hot water to boil away—Time's Arrow is guided in that direction by the second law. But wait! Steam can and often does condense to form hot water—and the Arrow has reversed its direction. Although at first one might think that considerations of this sort seriously limit the applicability of the second law, we shall soon see that this reversing character of Time's Arrow is at the root of many of the most useful applications of thermodynamics.

We shall both resolve and make use of the problem of the reversing Arrow by combining the first and second laws of thermodynamics. As a beginning we consider the equilibrium state in several simple systems for which our everyday experience provides helpful guides.

The first of these systems to consider is the familiar one consisting of ice and water. Suppose that we put some ice into some tap water. If the ice came out of the refrigerator, it was initially at some temperature lower than 0°C (equal to 32°F), while the tap water was at some temperature higher than 0°C. The warm water loses heat to the ice, thereby causing the temperature of the water to drop. At first the heat that the ice gains from the water goes to warming up the ice to 0°C. If this were all that happens, we could prepare cold drinks as well with cold iron cubes as with the more usual ice cubes. But when the ice reaches 0°C, the heat that the ice is receiving from the warm water no longer goes into increasing the temperature of the ice. Instead, the ice remains at 0°C and the heat gained from the water causes some of the ice to melt to yield water at 0°C, which then mixes with the warmer water and further cools (and dilutes) the drink. This process continues until we have both ice and all of the water at 0°C or until the ice is all melted.

If we originally added enough ice to cool all of the water to 0°C, we find that we ultimately have ice and water in equilibrium at this temperature. Understanding of this *equilibrium state* is sufficiently important that we shall consider it in detail.

Now let us imagine that we add ice to water in an insulated bottle that prevents unwanted transfer of heat to or from the surroundings. Once the ice and water reach equilibrium at 0°C, there will be no net change in the system—that is, the temperature, the amount of ice, and the amount of water will remain constant. Now suppose that we introduce some heat to our system of ice and water in equilibrium at 0°C, possibly by means of an electrical heater dipping into the insulated bottle. Does the temperature of the ice-water mixture begin to rise? Direct observation with a thermometer shows that the temperature remains constant at 0°C until all of the ice has melted. The temperature can begin to rise only after all of the ice is melted.

We might well do another experiment in which we replace the electrical heater with a cooling coil from a refrigerator. As the cooling coil extracts heat from the ice-water mixture, the temperature remains constant at 0°C until the last of the liquid water is frozen to ice—then the temperature can drop below 0°C.

Consideration of experiments like those described with ice and water shows that the equilibrium state and, more especially, transformations involving the equilibrium state are intimately connected with variables such as the temperature. And if we accept for the moment that the second law points from water to ice at temperatures below 0°C and from ice to water at higher temperatures, we see how this constant equilibrium temperature is maintained when heat is put into or taken out of the ice-water mixture. As heat is added to the mixture at any finite rate, it inevitably raises the temperature of some of the ice-water mixture to a bit above 0°C. According to the second law, ice must melt when heated to above 0°C or when in contact with water whose temperature is even slightly above 0°C. Each bit of ice that melts does so with absorption of heat from the surrounding ice-water mixture, thereby restoring the temperature to 0°C. If we know the number of calories required to melt 1 gram of ice (the ΔH of melting or fusion) and the number of calories introduced by the electrical heater, our faith in the first law permits us to balance the books on energy transfer by calculating the amount of ice that will melt.

Many years ago Gilbert N. Lewis, an American chemist, introduced the idea of "escaping tendency" in connection with the description of the equilibrium state and the direction of spontaneous processes. At 0°C, the escaping tendency of ice just balances the escaping tendency of water and the ice-water system is said to be in equilibrium. Above 0°C, the escaping tendency of ice is greater than that of water; consequently H_2O molecules spontaneously escape from the ice phase and join the liquid-water phase—that is, the ice melts. Below 0°C, the water has greater escaping tendency than ice, so water spontaneously freezes. These escaping tendencies that change with temperature are pictured in Figure 8–1. One of the important achievements of thermodynamics is the calculation of such curves.

Now let us consider the system consisting of liquid water and water vapor in terms of Lewis' escaping tendency. If we introduce

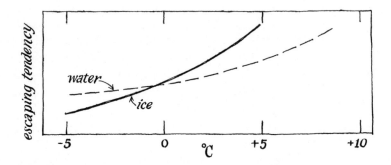

Figure 8–1. Below 0°C, water "escapes" to become ice. Above 0°C, ice "escapes" to become water.

some liquid water into a closed vessel maintained at some constant temperature, water will evaporate until the pressure of water vapor reaches some particular value. Then the system is in a state of equilibrium in which the escaping tendency of the liquid water just matches the pressure of the water vapor. Similar experiments at a series of different temperatures lead to results pictured in Figure 8–2.

Now we can begin to understand why hot water sometimes boils away and why steam sometimes condenses to hot water. Suppose that we have some hot water in a container in which there is some water vapor at any pressure lower than the equilibrium vapor pressure of water at the temperature of the water (say at point A in Figure 8–2). The escaping tendency of the water is greater than that of the water vapor at this temperature and pressure; hence the spontaneous process is the evaporation or boiling of the water. If the vessel is closed, this conversion of liquid water into water vapor will continue until the water vapor pressure reaches the equilibrium vapor pressure of the liquid water at this temperature (point E) so that the escaping tendencies are just equal. But if the container is open so that the water vapor can escape without building up to a higher pressure, all the water will evaporate away. On the other hand, when steam is cooled or compressed so

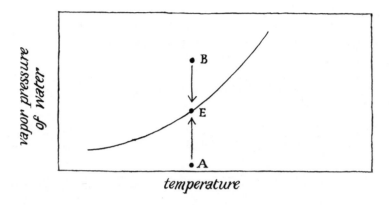

Figure 8–2. The curve indicates equilibrium vapor pressures of water over a range of temperature.

that its pressure is greater than the equilibrium vapor pressure of water at the final temperature of the steam (say at point *B*), the spontaneous process will be condensation of steam to liquid water —just the reverse of evaporation. This process will continue until the vapor pressure falls to point *E*.

The equilibrium vapor pressure of water at room temperature (about 20°C) is equivalent to a column of mercury 18 millimeters high. When we say that the relative humidity is 50 per cent, we mean that the actual vapor pressure of water vapor in the air is 50 per cent of the maximum the air can hold at this temperature without spontaneous condensation taking place. Thus the pressure of water vapor in the air is equivalent to 9 millimeters of mercury when the relative humidity is 50 per cent at 20°C. Since the vapor pressure of water at 20°C is greater than the pressure of the water vapor in the air at 50 per cent relative humidity, water at room temperature will spontaneously evaporate from a drinking glass. Then we might add some ice to the water and cool it to 0°C, where the equilibrium vapor pressure is equivalent to a column of mercury only 4.6 millimeters high. Since this pressure is less than the pressure of water vapor in the air, the spontaneous process is condensation of water vapor from the air to form cold water—the familiar droplets that form on a cold glass.

Solids also have equilibrium vapor pressures. Since we know that ice and water are in equilibrium at 0°C and have already pointed out that the equilibrium vapor pressure of water at 0°C is equivalent to 4.6 millimeters of mercury, it follows that the vapor pressure of ice at 0°C is also equivalent to 4.6 millimeters of mercury. If these vapor pressures were not equal, either ice or water would have the greater escaping tendency and they would not be in equilibrium at this temperature. From the spontaneous tendency of water to freeze below 0°C we know that water has a higher vapor pressure than ice below 0°C. Similarly, since ice spontaneously melts above 0°C, we know that ice must have a higher vapor pressure than water in this temperature range.

Now we can see why sometimes ice or snow spontaneously forms in the atmosphere and falls to the ground, while at other times snow or ice on the ground spontaneously evaporates (usually called sublimation for solids). Suppose that the temperature is −10°C, at which temperature the equilibrium vapor pressure of ice is equivalent to 2 millimeters of mercury. If the pressure of water vapor in the air is greater than this equilibrium pressure (possibly because warm, damp air has moved in from another area), ice or snow will form spontaneously. But if the air is sufficiently dry so that the pressure of water vapor in the air is less than 2 millimeters of mercury, ice or snow on the ground will spontaneously vaporize.

All of the examples of reversible processes considered in the preceding section can proceed in one way (under certain conditions) with evolution of heat and in the other way (under different conditions) with absorption of heat. Our first step toward understanding this reversible character of Time's Arrow involves consideration of the relation between probability and entropy. Even though most of us have never performed experiments with mixtures of red and green balls in a bucket, we all know by common sense what will happen. Although common sense casually applied is often a misleading substitute for true scientific thought and experiment, this time it does give us a useful guide.

Suppose that we put a layer of green balls in the bottom of a bucket and then cover this layer with a layer of red balls. Shaking the bucket will give us two layers that contain roughly equal numbers of red and green balls. Further shaking is extremely unlikely to result in a return to one layer of green balls and another layer of red balls.

We can also predict correctly that if we first fill a sack with red and green balls and then reach into the sack (no peeking) to obtain balls to place one by one in the bottom layer and then in the top layer, we will end up with layers each containing roughly equal numbers of red and green balls.

In the language of thermodynamics, we say that in each case we end up with layers of mixed colors rather than layers of single colors because the former is a state of higher probability or entropy than the latter. Since the reverse process of unmixing the colors is so unlikely as to be practically impossible, we might conclude that disorder or randomness (entropy) cannot decrease by itself. This generalization is a crude statement of the second law of thermodynamics.

The same principle applies to chemical reactions as can be seen by considering the reaction

$$H_2 + D_2 \rightleftarrows 2\,HD$$

In this expression H_2 represents "ordinary" hydrogen, each molecule of which consists of two atoms of ordinary hydrogen bound together. Similarly, D_2 represents "heavy" hydrogen (deuterium), each molecule of which consists of two deuterium atoms bound together. HD represents the mixed hydrogen in which each molecule is made up of one atom of ordinary hydrogen bound to one atom of heavy hydrogen. The double arrow symbol indicates that the reaction may under certain conditions proceed in either direction.

In converting $H_2 + D_2$ into 2 HD, H—H bonds and D—D bonds are broken while H—D bonds are formed. As might be expected in this case, the energy absorbed in breaking bonds is almost exactly balanced by the energy liberated in forming other bonds; thus the energy change in this reaction is nearly zero.

Now if we recognize that there is no energy difference between layers of mixed green and red balls and layers containing balls of only one color, we also recognize a similarity between our earlier discussion and the present problem of reaction in the H_2-D_2-HD chemical system. The direction of Time's Arrow and the equilibrium state to which the Arrow points should both be determined by probability considerations.

When a mole (remember that a mole is 6×10^{23} molecules) of H_2 is mixed with a mole of D_2, about half of each reacts with the other to form HD (left to right in the reaction equation) because a mixture of HD, D_2, and H_2 has more entropy (randomness or disorder) than does a mixture of only D_2 and H_2. Similarly, if one started with two moles of pure HD, about half would decompose (right to left in the reaction equation) so that the composition of the resulting mixture has the same proportions of H_2, D_2, and HD as the mixture obtained from H_2 and D_2 as starting materials. In both cases the reaction proceeds spontaneously until it reaches a state of equilibrium, which is a state of maximum entropy for this system. A graph of entropy vs composition for the H_2-D_2-HD system is shown in Figure 8–3. In this graph, X marks the composition corresponding to maximum entropy, which is also the equilibrium composition.

As pointed out in Chapter 7, one statement of the second law is that spontaneous processes in an isolated system must be accompanied by an increase in entropy. It therefore follows that the ultimate equilibrium state in such a system must be the state of

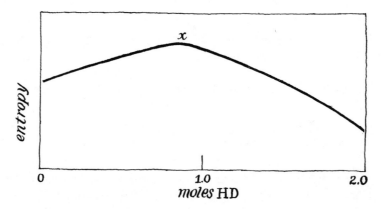

Figure 8–3. Graph of entropy *vs.* composition for the H_2-D_2-HD system made by mixing one mole of H_2 with one mole of D_2 or by starting with two moles of HD. The system has maximum entropy in the equilibrium state marked by X where it consists of about one-half mole each of H_2 and D_2 and about one mole of HD.

maximum entropy, since all other states will change to the equilibrium state with increase of entropy but the equilibrium state can change to other states only with a forbidden decrease of entropy.

For general treatment of nonisolated systems we later consider energy along with entropy in locating the equilibrium state. But for the green and red ball system, the H_2-D_2-HD system and other systems in which there are no significant energy effects in going from one state to another, it is necessarily only the entropy of the system that determines the equilibrium state. Thus if we start with any mixture of H_2, D_2, and HD other than the equilibrium mixture of maximum entropy, we see that spontaneous reactions must proceed to the equilibrium state with the increase of entropy demanded by the second law. Once the system reaches the equilibrium state of maximum entropy, no further change can be spontaneous since any change from this state would have to be accompanied by a forbidden decrease in entropy.

We have already seen some instances of the utility of statements of the second law in terms of the increase in entropy of an isolated system. But for many purposes we are much more interested in systems that are not isolated—that is, systems in contact with their environment so that both energy and entropy changes must be considered. Our approach to this problem is an extension of a discussion by American biologist Harold F. Blum in his book *Time's Arrow and Evolution.*

We will be concerned with the equilibrium distributions of idealized Mexican jumping beans [1] between adjoining compartments in boxes. Our idealized jumping beans are supposed to be jumping randomly with respect to both height and direction.

Suppose that a number of beans are placed in compartment 1 in Figure 8–4a. A bean will occasionally jump from compartment 1 to compartment 2. At first more beans will jump from 1 to 2 because more beans are in 1 than in 2. For as long as there are more beans in compartment 1 than in 2, net transfer of beans from 1 to 2 is a spontaneous process that brings the system closer to its equilibrium state. Since the wall height is the same for beans going in either direction and since the compartments are the same size, we know that equilibrium will be attained when the same number of beans are in each compartment. Equal distribution of the beans between the two compartments corresponds to a state of maximum probability and entropy. The reasoning we have used in considering this system is just the same as the reasoning we used in considering entropy and equilibrium in systems involving red and green balls and H_2-D_2-HD.

Next consider the equilibrium distribution of beans in Figure 8–5, which depicts a box with compartment 2 twice as big as compartment 1. Simple statistics tell us that the most probable

[1] *Mexican jumping beans are plant seeds with moth larvae enclosed. Movement of a larva causes a bean to move. When a bean is warmed, the vigorous wiggling of a larva causes the bean to jump a little.*

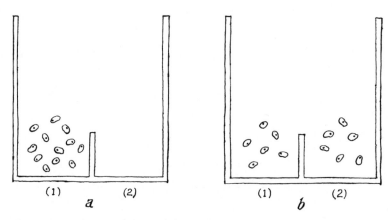

Figure 8–4. Illustration (a) shows the distribution when beans are first put into compartment 1. Illustration (b) shows the distribution after the beans have attained equilibrium. Note that the equilibrium distribution is attained whether the beans are initially in compartment 1 or 2 or in any nonequilibrium distribution between the compartments.

arrangement, hence the distribution corresponding to maximum entropy and the equilibrium state, is the one in which there are twice as many beans in large compartment 2 as in small compartment 1. Or we might reach the same conclusion by recognizing that the equilibrium state is attained when the rate of transfer of beans from 1 to 2 is just matched by the rate of transfer from 2 to 1 so that there is no net change in the distribution. Since compartment 2 is twice as large as compartment 1, the probability that a single bean will jump from 2 and land in 1 is only half the probability that a bean will jump from 1 and land in 2. In order to match the rates of transfer it is therefore necessary to have twice as many beans in 2 as in 1.

Our discussion of jumping beans as analogs of molecules has been designed partly to show that the equilibrium state is a state in which there is no net charge, but is not a static state. Rather, the equilibrium state is that state in which the escaping tendencies of the beans from adjoining compartments are equal. Rates of

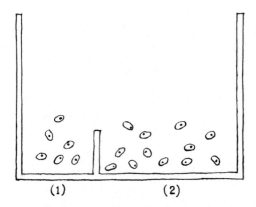

Figure 8–5. Equilibrium distribution of jumping beans when compartment 2 is twice as large as compartment 1. The density of beans (number of beans per square inch of compartment floor) is the same in each compartment.

transfer of beans in the two possible directions are equal so that there is no net change from the equilibrium distribution, although individual beans are hopping back and forth. There is ample evidence from experiments with radioactive tracers that the equilibrium state in a more conventional chemical system is also a state of dynamic equilibrium in which there is no net change, since rates of reaction in opposite directions are equal to each other at equilibrium. For instance, in a saturated (equilibrium) solution of sugar in water, the rate at which molecules of sugar dissolve from the solid into the solution is just matched by the rate at which molecules of sugar precipitate from the solution and join the solid.

Now let us consider distribution of beans in compartments arranged so that energy effects become important, as in Figure 8–6. Since compartment 2 is lower than 1, the barrier is much easier to jump over for beans going from compartment 1 to 2 than for beans going from compartment 2 to 1. Rates of transfer will be the same in both directions and we will have the equilibrium distribution

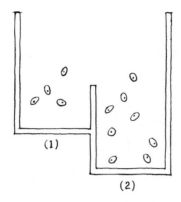

Figure 8–6. Equilibrium distribution of jumping beans between compartments of equal size, but at different heights. The density of beans is greater in the lower compartment than in the higher compartment.

only when there are more beans in the low compartment 2 than in the high compartment 1.

Conclusions that may be reached from our discussions of jumping beans may be summarized as follows: Energy effects tend to make the equilibrium distribution one in which most beans are in the *lower* compartment, while entropy effects tend to make most beans be in the *larger* compartment. We have reached these conclusions by considering special arrangements of compartments so that energy and entropy effects could be considered one at a time. This artificial separation is a reasonable and useful way to start, but ultimate application to real processes in the world around us requires that we consider systems in which both energy and entropy effects are important.

We might have compartments arranged so that the largest is also the lowest, as in Figure 8–7. In this case both energy and entropy effects favor an equilibrium distribution with most of the jumping beans in the larger, lower compartment, as shown in the illustration.

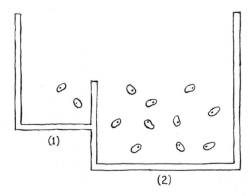

Figure 8–7. Both energy and entropy effects favor an
equilibrium distribution with most of the jumping beans
in the large, lower compartment.

But it is much more common to have energy and entropy effects
opposing each other as when the upper compartment is larger
than the lower compartment. Depending on relative elevations
and sizes of the compartments and jumping abilities of the beans,
the equilibrium distribution might have more beans in either
compartment or even the same number in each, as illustrated in
Figure 8–8.

Now let us consider the relation between jumping beans and
chemical reactions. To do so we must state once again that the
equilibrium distribution of beans between compartments does not
depend on whether we first put the beans in compartment 1 or in
compartment 2 or even whether we put some in each compartment. So suppose that we put all of the beans initially in the left-
side compartment, labeled LSC, and consider their eventual
distribution between this compartment and the right-side compartment, labeled RSC. A sort of "chemical reaction equation"
can thus be written

$$\text{LSC beans} \rightleftarrows \text{RSC beans}$$

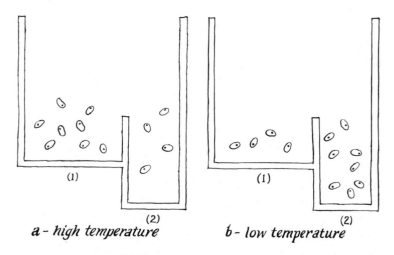

a - high temperature   **b - low temperature**

Figure 8–8. At high temperatures (beans jumping vigorously) the difference in barrier height for beans going from (1) to (2) or from (2) to (1) is not very important and the densities of beans in (1) and (2) are nearly equal. But the entropy effect (compartment size) requires that the total number of beans be greater in the larger compartment (1) as in (a). At low temperatures (beans are sluggish) the effect of barrier height is much greater and the density of beans in the lower compartment is so much greater than the density of beans in the higher compartment that the total number of beans in the smaller compartment may actually be greater than the number of beans in the larger compartment, as in (b).

We can express the equilibrium distribution of beans between the compartments in terms of an "equilibrium constant" analogous to similar expressions for chemical reactions. This equilibrium constant K is the ratio of the number of beans in the RSC to the number of those in the LSC at equilibrium, as indicated by

$$K = \frac{(\text{RSC})}{(\text{LSC})}$$

in which (LSC) and (RSC) represent the number of beans in each compartment. When this equilibrium constant K is a large number, most of the beans are in the RSC. Similarly, K near one corresponds to a nearly equal distribution of beans between the compartments, while very small K corresponds to most of the beans in the LSC.

It is customary to write chemical reaction equations with the reactant chemicals on the left side and the product chemicals on the right side. Thus,

$$\text{reactant chemicals} \rightleftarrows \text{product chemicals}$$

And just as for jumping beans, the equilibrium constant is a ratio of some measure of the amount of products to the amount of reactants remaining at equilibrium. A large value of K indicates that the reaction is one that proceeds largely to products, while a very small value of K indicates that the reaction proceeds only slightly to products so that most of the chemicals remain as unreacted reactants. By regarding a chemical reaction as a process in which some of the chemicals move from the "reactant compartment" to the "product compartment," we can easily extend our discussion of jumping beans to the important problem of chemical equilibrium.

We could now follow the pioneering thermodynamicists and derive equations that relate K to energy, entropy, and temperature. Because of the important work by Lewis and others in clarifying and applying the results first obtained by Helmholtz, van't Hoff, and especially Gibbs, derivation of these equations in textbooks of thermodynamics is easy. But we shall merely write down one equation and then explain and apply it. The "answers" that we want are all included in the equation

$$R \ln K = -\frac{\Delta H^0}{T} + \Delta S^0$$

In this equation $\ln K$ is the natural logarithm of the equilibrium constant K and R is a positive numerical constant. For qualitative understanding it is only necessary to know that a positive $\ln K$ corresponds to K greater than 1.0 while a negative $\ln K$ corresponds to K less than 1.0. The superscript zeros relate to ways of expressing amounts or concentrations of chemicals involved and are of considerable importance in detailed numerical calculations but need not concern us here.

We see that negative ΔH^0 and positive ΔS^0 correspond to positive ln K and thence to large K. Since negative ΔH^0 corresponds to a reaction that yields heat or to transfer of jumping beans from a high to a low compartment, a reaction of this sort is analogous to the transfer of beans from left to right, as pictured in Figure 8–7, in which both energy and entropy effects act in the same direction. Chemical reactions with all possible combinations of positive and negative ΔH^0 and ΔS^0 values are known and lead to both positive and negative ln K values and thence to both large and small equilibrium constants.

The "answers" equation tells us how equilibrium constants vary with temperature. When ΔH^0 is negative, increasing temperature T causes ln K and thence K to decrease. On the other hand, with positive ΔH^0, increasing T causes ln K and K to increase. We illustrate these effects by graphs in which values of K are plotted against the absolute temperature T as in Figure 8–9.

The relation between equilibrium constant and temperature given by the equation and shown graphically in Figure 8–9 is of great practical importance in such diverse fields as the production of useful substances from petroleum and the extraction of metals from their ores. We illustrate application of this relation by consideration of the fixation of nitrogen—that is, the chemical combination of atmospheric nitrogen with other elements to yield useful substances.

The equilibrium constant for the reaction of nitrogen with oxygen to form nitric oxide (chemical formula NO) is *much* less than 1.0 at ordinary temperature. This means that the reaction of nitrogen with oxygen cannot yield any appreciable amount of nitric oxide under these conditions. But we know from the enthalpy of nitric oxide that ΔH for the formation reaction is positive. According to the equation or the graph on the right side of Figure 8–9, the equilibrium constant for this reaction must increase with increasing temperature. By increasing the temperature to 2500°K this equilibrium constant is increased to about 0.1, which is large enough to permit appreciable reaction of nitrogen and oxygen to yield nitric oxide.

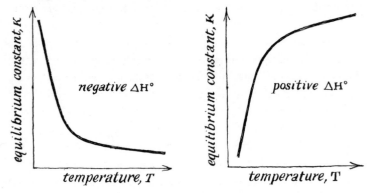

Figure 8–9. These graphs summarize the dependence of equilibrium constants on enthalpies (heats) of reaction.

This useful reaction of nitrogen with oxygen has been carried out in electric arcs, primarily in Norway where the product was used to make calcium nitrate for use as fertilizer sold under the name Norwegian saltpeter. More recently, this high-temperature reaction of nitrogen with oxygen has been carried out in gas-heated furnaces in the United States. Once the nitric oxide is produced by the very high-temperature reaction in the arc or furnace, it is cooled in the presence of excess oxygen with which it then reacts to form nitrogen dioxide (chemical formula NO_2). It is again thermodynamics in the form of our equation that tells us the proper temperature range for this second reaction, which cannot proceed to an appreciable extent at the high temperatures suitable for the first reaction. The nitrogen dioxide is ordinarily dissolved in water to form nitric acid and is then used in the manufacture of compounds ranging from fertilizers to explosives.

Some of the nitrogen and oxygen in air react to form nitric oxide when they are heated by a bolt of lightning. As the nitric oxide cools, it reacts further with oxygen to form nitrogen dioxide and then dissolves in water to form a dilute solution of nitric acid. The amount of nitric acid formed in this way commonly amounts to one to ten pounds per acre per year in regions of moderate rainfall and is an important factor in maintaining soil quality.

Nowadays many people are becoming interested in the important social, political, and military consequences of scientific developments. In this connection it is interesting to consider the work of Fritz Haber, a German Jew, on the production of ammonia. Largely thermodynamic considerations led Haber (important contributions were also made by Nernst, Bosch, and a few others) to a successful process for manufacture of ammonia after such competent workers as Le Chatelier and Ramsay had tried and failed.

Calculations with the equilibrium constant equation given earlier show that the equilibrium constant for formation of ammonia (NH_3) from nitrogen and hydrogen is a little larger than 800 at ordinary temperature ($298°K = 25°C = 77°F$). But at this temperature the rate of reaction is so slow that in practice no ammonia at all can be produced. At higher temperatures the rate of reaction increases markedly, but the positive ΔH^0 for the reaction requires that the equilibrium constant for formation must decrease as the temperature increases. Haber worked out a practical compromise between the good yield associated with a large equilibrium constant at low temperature and a reasonable rate of reaction at high temperature. After several years of theoretical and experimental work, Haber demonstrated in 1905 that he could make a workable process and then in 1908 he took out a key patent on his process.

Before Haber's work, nearly all of the fixed nitrogen used for fertilizers and in industrial chemical processes came from Chilean saltpeter. Because of the rising population of the world, increased food production with the aid of fertilizers (almost all made from saltpeter) was becoming of greater and greater importance. But it was really World War I that concentrated attention on industrial fixation of nitrogen. All of the explosives (TNT, guncotton, dynamite, etc.) used in guns and bombs prior to Hiroshima required nitric acid for their manufacture, and before World War I this nitric acid came from saltpeter.

In 1909 the *Badische Anilin und Sodafabrik* began work on industrial production of ammonia by means of Haber's process. This ammonia could be used directly as liquid fertilizer, allowed to react with acids to yield solid fertilizers, or reacted with oxygen in the Ostwald process to yield nitric acid. Production of ammonia in Germany in 1913 amounted to about 7,000 tons and roughly doubled in each following year until it reached 200,000 tons per year at the end of the war. Since the naval blockade effectively prevented Germany from importing saltpeter, it was the ammonia produced by the Haber process that enabled Germany to continue its war effort and saved the country from premature defeat. Leonard Nash, an American chemist, has written:

> Is it a blessing to be so saved? Prolongation of the war so depleted Germany, and so embittered her foes, that the postwar situation may be thought to have made inevitable the rise of a Hitler. If this be so, the Haber process was no blessing for Germany, and certainly no blessing for Haber, who, with the rise of Hitler, became the "Jew-Haber" driven to his death in exile.

Here it might also be added that Haber developed a scheme for extracting gold from seawater with the aim of paying the German war debt. Although his scheme was very clever, it could not be made to produce gold cheaply enough to be of value. The essential difficulty was a matter of entropy. Concentrating gold from large volumes of seawater into nuggets involves a huge decrease in entropy. Such a process can occur only if there is an even larger increase in entropy in the environment, which can be achieved by burning enough coal or using enough electrical power.

Now let us turn to consideration of the third law of thermodynamics, which permits numerical evaluation of entropies of substances and is intimately connected with the statistical interpretation of entropy. Probably the most important single use of entropy data is in calculations with the equation for K. From the entropies of chemical substances it is a simple matter to calculate the ΔS^0 values to be used with ΔH^0 values derived from enthalpies of these same substances. Part of the importance of this sort of calculation is that it permits one to know an equilibrium constant for a reaction without having actually investigated the reaction itself at all. If the equilibrium constant is small, the reaction is one that ordinarily cannot proceed usefully under the conditions relevant to the calculation. But if the equilibrium constant is large and no reaction is observed when the chemicals are mixed, there is at least a possibility that a useful catalyst can be found to speed up the attainment of equilibrium.

We can understand something of the statistical nature of entropy by considering the sharing of energy between a group of particles in systems of specified temperature and total energy. By choosing a system containing only a few particles and in which the allowed energy levels are equally spaced, we can make these considerations both simple and brief.

First, we consider the sharing of energy between three particles in a system with equally spaced energy levels, each with an energy that is an integral multiple of energy ϵ. The lowest level (our "sea level" of energy) has energy $0 \times \epsilon = 0$, the next level has energy ϵ, the next has energy $2\,\epsilon$, etc. If we fix the total energy of the system, it immediately follows that only certain distributions of the three particles among the various energy levels are possible because only certain distributions will have the right total energy.

For instance, when the total energy is fixed at ϵ, we must have one particle in the level with energy ϵ and the other two particles in the zero energy level as pictured in Figure 8–10.

Figure 8–10. Distribution of three particles having total energy ϵ.

We have no reason to think that any of the distributions shown in Figure 8–10 is either more or less probable than any other distribution (always restricting our considerations to those distributions that have the assigned total energy). We therefore make the reasonable assumption, which may be regarded as the fundamental axiom of statistical mechanics, that these distributions are equally probable. Thus if we could observe this group of molecules at many different times, we would find each of the three pictured distributions occurring equally often. Or we might observe many such systems once, in which case we would find that equal numbers of systems would have each of the pictured distributions.

Now let us consider the possible distributions of three particles when the total energy is $2\,\epsilon$, corresponding to a higher temperature than in the previous example. In this case we may have one particle in the $2\,\epsilon$ level and two particles in the zero energy level or have two particles in the ϵ level and one particle in the zero energy level. Each of these arrangements can be realized in three ways, leading to the six possible distributions pictured in Figure 8–11. Since these distributions are all equally probable, we only need to count the dots in each level to know the relative populations of the various levels. In the lowest level we find 9, in the next level (ϵ) we find 6 and in the highest occupied level ($2\,\epsilon$) we find 3.

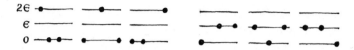

Figure 8–11. Distribution of three particles having total energy 2 ε.

As our last example of this sort, we consider the possible distributions of three particles when the total energy is 3 ε. All three particles might have energy ε, which is an arrangement that can be realized in only one way. We might also have one particle in the 3 ε level and the other two in the zero energy level. This arrangement can be realized in three ways. Or we might have one particle in each of the three lowest levels, an arrangement that can be realized in six ways. All of these distributions are shown in Figure 8–12. Since these distributions are all equally probable,

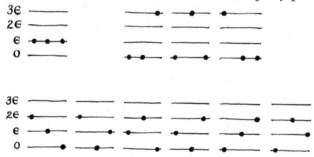

Figure 8–12. Distribution of three particles having total energy 3 ε.

we count the dots in the various levels to learn that relative populations are 12 in the lowest level, 9 in the next level, 6 in the next level, and 3 in the highest level that is occupied.

The three examples that we have considered so far illustrate the general principle that the lowest level is the most populated, with each higher energy level having a smaller population than the level below it. Further detailed considerations of this sort can lead to the Boltzmann distribution equation, which is the basis for numerical calculations of entropies of gases and certain other systems. But for our present purpose, it is sufficient merely to consider the number of allowed distributions.

At the low temperature corresponding to total energy ϵ (Figure 8–10) there are only three possible distributions. For this same system at the higher temperature corresponding to total energy 2ϵ (Figure 8–11), there are six possible distributions, while at the still higher temperature corresponding to total energy 3ϵ (Figure 8–12) there are ten possible distributions. Boltzmann's relation between entropy and number of allowed distributions, which is often called a relation between entropy and probability, tells us that the entropy increases as the number of distributions increases. Thus the entropy also increases as the temperature increases.

Although we would use the Boltzmann relation for detailed calculations relating number of distributions to entropy, we can explain the general connection in other terms. If a system can exist in any of a large number of distributions, we say that the state which includes these distributions is a highly probable one with considerable microscopic randomness or chaos, while a system that can exist in only a few distributions is in a state of lower randomness or chaos and thus also a state of lower entropy. We might also say that our ignorance of the distribution is greater for a high entropy state (many possible distributions) than for a low entropy state (few possible distributions). Thus increased entropy corresponds to decreased information about the microscopic distribution of a system. Considerations of this latter sort are the basis for the "information theory" that is of considerable importance in communications and that Myron Tribus believes will be proved to be a logical basis for both classical and statistical thermodynamics.

The specific heat (generally refers to one gram of substance) or heat capacity (generally refers to one mole of substance) is a measure of the relation between added energy and corresponding temperature increase of a system. Thus measured heat capacities can be used in calculating the entropy change associated with heating a system from one temperature to another. This is possibly the principal reason that "old-fashioned" measurements of this sort are still of considerable importance and attract the attention of many scientists and engineers.

As the temperature of a system decreases, both the total energy of the system and the number of possible microscopic distributions decrease. At the absolute zero of temperature ($0°K$), the energy is as low as it can get and the only possible distribution for our system of three particles is that pictured in Figure 8–13.

Figure 8–13. Only distribution of three particles having lowest possible energy at absolute zero of temperature.

Thus we can say that we have no uncertainty or ignorance about the distribution of this system and the entropy is therefore zero at the absolute zero of temperature. Similarly, Boltzmann's logarithmic relation between entropy and number of distributions says that the entropy is zero when there is only one possible distribution (remember that the logarithm of one is zero).

Although the third law of thermodynamics has been stated in a number of rigorous ways, we can extract the general sense of them all in the following statement: *The entropy of a system in equilibrium is zero at the absolute zero of temperature.* This law had its origins in the work of W. H. Nernst in Germany, who was concerned with applications of the previously cited equation relating ΔS^0 and ΔH^0 to the equilibrium constant. This work led him to formulate the Nernst heat theorem, which can be regarded as the immediate forerunner of the third law. Subsequent investigations by others, including Theodore Richards, Max Planck, Gilbert N. Lewis, and especially Giauque, have firmly established the third law so that in 1952 Sir Francis Simon wrote "The third law of thermodynamics is today the most important guiding principle in low temperature research."

Just as the first and second laws can be stated in terms of the impossibility of doing certain things, the third law may be stated in terms of the impossibility of reaching the absolute zero by means of any finite number of steps. This statement immediately raises questions about how close one can get and what sorts of methods can be used to get as close to absolute zero as possible.

Since the mid-nineteenth century considerable effort has been expended on developing new or better ways of achieving lower and lower temperatures. Many of the early efforts made use of the Joule-Thomson effect or various machines that operated on much the same principles as our present refrigerators and were primarily concerned with liquefying nitrogen, oxygen, etc. As a result of this work, much of which involved clever applications of thermodynamics, it ultimately became possible to liquefy helium. The normal boiling point of liquid helium is 4.2°K. A liquid boils when its vapor pressure equals the applied pressure: thus the normal boiling point is the boiling temperature when the pressure is normal atmospheric pressure. As the pressure is decreased with a vacuum pump or by going up a mountain, the temperature required to attain an equivalent vapor pressure drops and the observed boiling temperature also drops. With the best possible vacuum pumps it has been possible to achieve a pressure low enough to lower the boiling point of helium to about 1°K. No further progress was even in sight until 1926 when William F. Giauque and Peter Debye independently worked out the principle of adiabatic demagnetization. The word "adiabatic" comes from the Greek and means no heat flow.

To understand this method, we consider the entropy of an appropriate magnetic material in a magnetic field and in the absence of a magnetic field. Since the effect of the applied magnetic field is to orient (remove randomness) the little "atomic magnets" in the substance, the substance has lower entropy in the presence of the field than in the absence of the field, as shown in Figure 8–14. Now suppose that we start with an unmagnetized sample of material immersed in liquid helium that is boiling at the particular pressure of the experiment. If we now apply a strong magnetic field to our sample, the "atomic magnets" are lined up and the entropy decreases. The temperature is maintained constant because of the contact of the sample with the boiling helium: the energy of magnetization is dissipated by boiling away more helium without causing the temperature to rise. By this constant temperature magnetization process, our sample of material is changed from the state represented by A to that represented by B in Figure 8–14.

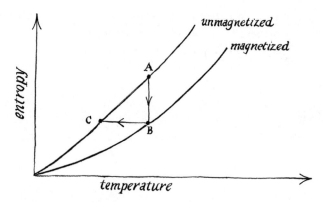

Figure 8–14. Illustration of the magnetic method for reaching the lowest attainable temperature.

Next we remove the liquid helium in such fashion that our magnetized material is isolated from its surroundings so that no heat can flow into or out of our substance. Once we have our magnetized substance properly isolated from its surroundings, we turn off the magnet and allow the "atomic magnets" to return to their normal state of random orientation, which corresponds to the upper line in Figure 8–14. Now it is one of the consequences of the second law that a process of this sort proceeds without change in entropy of the isolated substance, corresponding to moving from point B to point C in Figure 8–14. Thus we have succeeded in lowering the temperature from A to C by this constant temperature magnetization-adiabatic demagnetization process. It is by techniques of this sort that temperatures close to $0.000001°K$ have been achieved and many detailed measurements on the properties of solids below $1°K$ have been made.

One might well ask the following question: If it is possible to cool a substance from room temperature to $4.2°$ to $1°$ to $0.000001°K$, just *why* can't we go the rest of the way to the absolute zero. The third law gives the answer to this question in terms of the disappearing entropy, which means that at sufficiently low temperatures there is no significant amount of entropy to be lost on magnetization. An answer in more familiar terms is given by the old story about a frog hopping to the well to get a drink. This imaginary frog jumps half the *remaining* distance to the well with each hop. How many hops does it take for the frog to reach the well? Of course the answer is that the frog never quite gets to the well at all, and so it is with the approach to absolute zero.

chapter nine
demons,
poetry,
and life

Though the second law of thermodynamics is considerably more subtle than the first law, man has recognized its ubiquity for thousands of years and has reflected this recognition in his folklore.

> Humpty Dumpty sat on a wall
> Humpty Dumpty had a great fall!
> All the king's horses
> And all the king's men
> Couldn't put Humpty Dumpty together again.

There is historical evidence that this nursery rhyme is one of those pieces of antiquity that is dated in the thousands of years. Humpty Dumpty has his counterparts in France (*Boule-boule*), Sweden (*Thille Lille*), Denmark (*Lille-Trille*), Finland (*Hillerin-Lillerin*) and Germany (*Hümpelken-Pümpelken*). Experiences of catastrophic irreversibility such as those described in the ancient English rhyme form a part of man's universal heritage of trouble. The proverbs of the world are rich in spilt milk, burnt boats, and wasted youth. Each of these proverbs can be regarded as a statement of the second law, which expresses the unidirectionality of life and the utter futility of expecting a second chance.[1]

[1] *Myron Tribus, an American professor of engineering, while lecturing on the second law, remarked that "The entropy of any system can be decreased at the expense of some other body. There is no process that cannot be reversed if we are willing to accept*

Figure 9–1. . . . All the king's horses
And all the king's men
Couldn't put Humpty Dumpty together again.

The second law has been assaulted many times. No assault has been more persistent nor been taken more seriously than the one initiated in 1871 by James Clerk Maxwell, a brilliant Scottish physicist. Maxwell suggested that an intelligent being small enough to deal with the motions of individual molecules would be capable of violating the second law. Consider an isolated enclosure that initially contains a gas at a uniform temperature. The enclosure is divided into two sections by a partition with a small

a greater irreversibility somewhere else." A member of the audience asked, "How do you unscramble an egg?" The answer, "Feed it to a chicken."

door in it. Maxwell imagined the existence of a small intelligent being, called a demon, who would open and close the door to permit molecules with greater than average velocities to pass from left to right and to permit molecules with less than average velocities to pass from right to left. Figure 9–2 illustrates the

Figure 9–2. Maxwell's demon. The demon is effectively blind in this situation.

demon at work. You will recall that the higher the mean speed of the molecules making up a gas, the higher the gas temperature. In this way the gas in the right-hand half of the enclosure would become hotter and the gas in the left-hand compartment colder, all without the expenditure of any energy. Once the temperature difference was established, it could be used to drive a heat engine that would deliver useful work.

Perpetual motion machines of the second kind (so-called because they would violate the second law) attempt to get work from thermal energy on hand, without the required difference in intensity factor. That is, they are attempts to get work out of thermal energy already at the temperature of the surroundings. Alas, the second law forbids these devices. But let us get back to Maxwell and his demon to see what he had in mind.

At this point we remind the reader why Maxwell's device is a so-called perpetual motion machine of the second kind. Maxwell's device, if it were able to operate, would obtain work from a reservoir that was initially at a uniform temperature. Let us contemplate the advantages of machines that could violate the second law in this way. Ocean-going vessels, for example, could take in seawater at the bow, extract energy from the water to maintain steam in its boilers, and discharge chunks of ice at the stern. Who could object, except possibly the Coast Guard or fuel-oil producers?

There is no question that Maxwell was willing to endow his demon with superordinary powers. He supposed that his demon would be able to sense the velocity (speed and direction) of individual molecules and then act accordingly. If the demon had been invented yesterday rather than nearly a hundred years ago, we do not believe he would have created such a stir. Léon M. Brillouin, a French physicist, asked and answered the really fundamental question: *Is it actually possible for the demon to see the individual molecules?*

As the demon peers into either side of the isolated enclosure at uniform temperature, the uniformity of radiation throughout does not permit him to see anything. The sameness in the enclosure would allow him to perceive the thermal radiation (and its fluctuations), but he would never see the molecules. It is not surprising that Maxwell did not think of including radiation in his scheme since he proposed the demon thirty years before the thermodynamics of radiation was clearly understood.

We conclude that the demon needs his own supply of light to disturb the radiation equilibrium within the enclosure, so we equip him with a flashlight to enable him to see the molecules. The flashlight is a source of radiation not in equilibrium. The energy that the flashlight pours into the system provides the demon with the information that he needs to operate the door to separate the high-speed molecules from the low-speed ones. If we divide the radiant energy emitted by the bulb filament by the temperature of the filament, we calculate a quantity which we call negative entropy. (Brillouin suggested calling it *negentropy*.) It is this negentropy that permits the demon to obtain information about the speed and location of the molecules. It can be shown, however, that the over-all increase in entropy will be greater than any local entropy decrease that the demon can cause with his separating efforts. That is, for the *entire* system of flashlight, demon, and gas, there will be a net entropy increase just as the second law requires.

Negentropy measures the quality of energy. A system contains negentropy if it has a possibility of doing work. Systems not at a uniform temperature throughout, not at a uniform pressure throughout, or not at a uniform electrical potential can all do work and thus all contain certain amounts of negentropy.

Thus when the demon shines the flashlight into the enclosure, he pours negentropy into it as is shown in Figure 9–3. From this

Figure 9–3. Maxwell's demon is now equipped with a flashlight which allows him to see the molecules and thus separate them.

negentropy the demon obtains information. Using this information, he operates the door, creates a temperature difference and therefore creates more negentropy, thus completing the cycle:

The concept of negentropy may be applied far and wide, even to the writing of poetry. Poets frequently do not say exactly what they mean: that is, they transmit a coded message. If the code is to be broken, the second law says that a price must be paid for the information. The author's message or information is intended for a select audience—those who can break the code. Negentropy must be spent by those readers capable of receiving the message. C. D. Nash, Jr., an American engineering professor of catholic interests, has pointed out that poets [2] have recognized either explicitly or implicitly the second law of thermodynamics. In "Mending Wall," Robert Frost wrote:

> . . . Before I built a wall I'd ask to know
> What I was walling in or walling out,
> And to whom I was like to give offense.
> Something there is that doesn't love a wall,
> That wants it down.' "I could say 'Elves' to him,
> But it's not elves exactly, and I'd rather
> He said it for himself. I see him there
> Bringing a stone grasped firmly by the top
> In each hand, like an old-stone savage armed. . . .

By expending some negentropy it is possible to break Frost's code and see that he has introduced (perhaps unknowingly) the second law of thermodynamics.

[2] *"Poets . . . say many fine things, but they understand nothing that they say." Socrates:* In Plato's Apology of Socrates.

The observer, whether he be natural philosopher, demon, or poetry reader, requires sources of negentropy since every observation is always made at the expense of the negentropy of the surroundings. He needs batteries, power supplies, foodstuffs, etc., all of which represent sources of negentropy. If he is supplied with these things, he can indeed operate the door, measure the velocity of a molecule, or understand a particular poem, but he has paid the price the second law demands. Thus we come to the conclusion reached by Dennis Gabor, a Hungarian-English physicist, "We cannot get anything for nothing, not even an observation." In a more rigorous form the second law can be stated thus: *Our information about an isolated system can never increase. Reversible processes conserve, irreversible ones lose information.* This statement implies that only by measurement can new information be obtained, but when we make a measurement on a system, it is no longer isolated. It should be made clear that information theory imposes a limit on the observations and measurements of a physical system over and above that imposed by the Heisenberg Uncertainty Principle.[3] Brillouin has shown that any information resulting from a physical observation must be paid for by an increase in entropy in the laboratory. This entropy increase, on the average, will be larger than the information obtained when they are both measured in the same system of units. It is this condition that represents a new limitation on the possibilities of observation.

[3] *The Heisenberg Uncertainty Principle imposes a fundamental limitation on the determination of an object's momentum and position. For example, to determine the location of a molecule in a gas with high precision would require a beam of light of high energy. The interaction of this light with the gas molecule would alter the molecule's momentum significantly. Hence, the molecule's position and momentum cannot both be determined simultaneously with unlimited precision.*

In a certain sense the development of civilization may appear contradictory to the second law. Man introduces order into his environment by building structures for shelter, transportation, education, and entertainment. All of these are creations of order out of disorder. A house is more than a pile of bricks; it is an orderly arrangement of component parts and thus represents a state of lower entropy than a pile of its parts. Man creates language, an orderly pattern of speech sounds and written signs. The communication of information from man to man replaces what would otherwise be chaos in relations between individuals. The social institutions of government, law, and education also reflect ways in which man has consciously tried to maximize the order in his environment and to reduce entropy as much as possible.

There are fluctuations in the entropy reduction caused by man. Antisocial behavior [4] that manifests itself in the destructive actions of certain human beings clearly assists the second law toward the final state of maximum chaos.

Some scholars recognize society itself as a force that tends to produce order out of disorder, thus producing large-scale, but local, entropy reductions. The ceaseless urge of man to bring order out of his experiences so that he may understand them gives rise to science, which is a relevant example of entropy reduction. Through experimentation he tests new ideas in a systematic way in a desire to obtain greater order in human experience.

Even though society can effect local reductions in entropy, the general and universal trend of entropy increase easily swamps the anomalous but important efforts of civilized man. Each localized, man-made or machine-made entropy decrease is accompanied by a greater increase in entropy of the surroundings, thereby maintaining the required increase in total entropy.

[4] *An arsonist working on a big library is merely speeding up the inevitable result demanded by the second law.*

Carl Sandburg recognized man's tendency to try to produce order from disorder, but he also recognized that it was a battle that man would lose sooner or later. His poem "Under" describes this battle.

I am the undertow
Washing tides of power
Battering the pillars
Under your things of high law.

I am a sleepless
Slowfaring eater,
Maker of rust and rot
In your bastioned fastenings,
Caissons deep.

I am the Law
Older than you
And your builders proud.

I am deaf
In all days
Whether you
Say "Yes" or "No."

I am the crumbler: tomorrow.

Another poem by Sandburg, "Limited," is one of the more explicit literary statements of the second law.

I am riding on a limited express, one of the crack trains of the nation.
Hurtling across the prairie into the blue haze and dark air go fifteen all-steel coaches holding a thousand people.

> (All the coaches shall be scrap and rust and all the men
> and women laughing in the diners and sleepers shall
> pass to ashes.)
> I ask a man in the smoker where he is going and he
> answers: "Omaha."

Statistical techniques for the calculation of entropy values are
now being applied to such nonrandom activities as writing. In this
case entropy is a statistical parameter that measures how much
unexpectedness is in a message source. As we have seen earlier,
entropy is related to the disorganization of a physical system.
Disorganization may be interpreted as meaning how little the
observer knows about the system. If an observer learns something
about a physical system, its entropy is decreased, since for him it
has become less disorganized. When an observer knows more
about a system, he can obtain work from it. As he learned about
the velocity of molecules approaching each side of the partition,
Maxwell's demon became capable of setting up a system that
would yield work.

The printed page may also be analyzed with respect to order
and disorder; this is done by calculating the probability of occur-
rence of a meaningful sequence of letters or symbols as a fraction
of the total number of different jumbles that could be put together from the same collection of letters and symbols. Such a
calculation can be expressed in terms of the negentropy or reduction of entropy that is effected by intelligent selection from a
random collection of letters. The entropies used in these calculations, unlike those associated with thermal energy, are defined as
dimensionless mathematical measures of these probabilities.
There are several ways of calculating entropies in linguistic situations, but they are somewhat involved.

A statistical analysis of the English language has been given by
Brillouin. For example, the probability of a word space or blank
occurring in written English is 0.2, the letter e has a probability

of 0.105, while the letters q and z have probabilities of only 0.001.

A more refined statistical analysis treats words as made up of component syllables, rather than component letters. Thus it is possible to compute the average number of syllables per word and then to relate this to the entropy. Wilhelm Fucks of Germany has examined quite a lot of literature in this way and come up with some interesting results. The accompanying table gives some of his results for six works in English, one in German, and one in Latin. We have also added some calculations of our own (starred) for comparative purposes. Most of the analyses done to date show that

Results of a Syllabic and Entropic Analysis of Certain Authors' Writings

author	work	average number of syllables per word	entropy
°Fleming	*Goldfinger*	1.26	0.28
Shakespeare	*Othello*	1.29	0.29
Galsworthy	*Forsyte Saga*	1.34	0.33
Huxley	*Antic Hay*	1.41	0.38
°Bellow	*Herzog*	1.47	0.40
°Churchill	*Their Finest Hour*	1.48	0.40
Thomas Mann	*Buddenbrooks*	1.74	0.51
Sallust	*Epistula, II*	2.48	0.64

when English, German, Greek, and Latin are compared, English shows the lowest entropy. One of the simplest interpretations that can be made of these calculations is that writings that have low values of entropy carry the most information per syllable.

Information theory techniques have also been applied to the problem of the origin of life on earth. Answers are obtained fairly directly, but because so many quantities have to be estimated the results are not quantitatively reliable.

Life, the temporary reversal of a universal trend toward maximum disorder, was brought about by the production of information mechanisms. In order for such mechanisms to first arise it was necessary to have matter capable of forming itself into a self-reproducing structure that could extract energy from the environment for its first self-assembly. Directions for the reproduction of plans, for extraction of energy and chemicals from the environment, for the growth sequence and the mechanism for translating instructions into growth *all* had to be simultaneously present at that moment. This combination of events has seemed an incredibly unlikely happenstance and often divine intervention is prescribed as the only way it could have come about.

People who play Russian roulette have a feeling that an event with a probability of $\frac{1}{6}$ can't happen—at least on the first chance. More rational people have the same general philosophy about unlikely events, although most of us like the probability of an unpleasant event to be much smaller than $\frac{1}{6}$. In our everyday life we are being reasonable when we regard an event with a probability of one part in a million million as so unlikely as to be impossible. But everyday notions of the impossibility of highly improbable events cannot be carried over into discussion of the origins of life. From a statistical point of view, life could have originated at any instant in a period of time longer than a billion years. Further, the origin of life was not limited to just one spot (unless it be the Garden of Eden), but could have begun almost anywhere on the earth. Under these conditions, an event with a probability of one part in a million million would have occurred many times, even though it is reasonable for us to regard such an event as presently impossible.

Many clever explanations have been developed to attempt to explain the original formation of the amino acids that are the immediate precursors of proteins and living matter. Some of these are based on the results of experiments conducted by Stanley Miller when he was a graduate student at the University of Chicago in 1952. He demonstrated that amino acids are produced when a mixture of ammonia, water, and methane is subjected to an electrical discharge. It is therefore possible that a bolt of lightning supplied the driving force for the first step toward life. Or it could be that some other source of negentropy, such as volcanic action, made possible the exceedingly improbable organization of atoms that was certainly necessary.

We are faced with the idea that genesis was a statistically unlikely event. We are also faced with the certainty that it occurred. Was there a temporary repeal of the second law that permitted a "fortuitous concourse of atoms"? If so, study of the Repealer and genesis is a subject properly left to theologians. Or we may hold with the more traditional scientific attitude that the origin of life is beclouded merely because we don't know enough about the composition of the atmosphere and other conditions on the earth many eons ago.

According to Brillouin, scientists can be divided into three groups, depending on the stand they take with regard to life and the second law. Briefly they are:

1. Our present knowledge of physics and chemistry is practically complete, and these physical concepts will enable us to explain life without the intervention of any special "life principle."

2. We acknowledge that life obeys all the known laws of physics and chemistry, but we feel that something more is needed before we can understand life. It matters not whether we call it "life principle" or something else.

3. Living organisms behave completely differently than inert matter. Their behavior cannot be understood without reference to a "life principle." Life is an exception to the second law and the new principle of life will have to explain events that are contrary to the second law.

The attitude of scientists in class 1 corresponds to the attitude held by many physicists in 1900, when common opinion was that everything was known and that future generations of scientists would only improve on the accuracy of the experiments and measure one or two more decimal places of the physical constants. This sense of complete understanding of a well-ordered world soon came crashing down with the birth of quantum theory and the theory of relativity and the discovery of radioactivity.

Attitude 2 seems to be more constructive and in general corresponds to the trend of scientific thought, while attitude 3, despite its radical position, is not much more than an exaggeration of attitude 2. After all, we have observed many discoveries that have led to new laws and so the idea that something new is required should not come as too much of a shock.

Clausius epitomized the fundamental principles of thermodynamics as we told you earlier (in German): "the energy of the world is constant; the entropy of the world increases to a maximum." If the first law says we cannot get something for nothing, the second law emphasizes that every time we do get something we reduce by a measurable amount the opportunity to get that something in the future. Ultimately, there will come a time when there will be no more "getting." This is the so-called "heat death," predicted by Clausius, when our universe will have reached a dead level of temperature, and though the total amount of energy will be the same as always there will be no way to use it. That is, there will be no way to produce a difference in temperature, voltage, or anything else in any part of the universe—the entropy will have reached its maximum value.[5] In *The Time Machine*, H. G. Wells in 1895 describes a voyage into the future by his Time Traveller as he visits the coast of what had been England:

> So I travelled, stopping ever and again, in great strides of a thousand years or more, drawn on by the mystery of the earth's fate, watching with a strange fascination the sun

[5] *Compare Franz Kafka's dictum: "In the fight between you and the world, back the world."*

grow larger and duller in the westward sky, and the life of the old earth ebb away. At last more than thirty million years hence, the huge red-hot dome of the sun had come to obscure nearly a tenth part of the darkling heavens . . . the red beach, save for its livid green liverworts and lichens, seemed lifeless. . . . A bitter cold assailed me. . . . There were fringes of ice along the sea margin, with drifting masses further out. . . . The darkness grew apace . . . From the edge of the sea came a ripple and whisper. Beyond these lifeless sounds the world was silent.

There is a class of experiences puzzling to some scientists but which have a very important bearing on the subject at hand. As we have noted earlier, the entropy of an isolated system must increase or at least remain constant. When entropy increases, the system is experiencing an irreversible transformation; if the isolated system undergoes a reversible transformation, its total entropy remains constant. The other case in which no entropy increase takes place is the case of substances in *unstable states*.

The carburetor in your automobile engine vaporizes some gasoline into an air stream and the mixture is introduced into the cylinders of the engine. The mixture is compressed, as shown in Figure 9–4, and nothing happens (assuming it is not compressed too much). As long as the mixture sits there waiting for the spark, none of its properties (pressure, temperature, density, and, of course, entropy) is changing. Then the spark jumps across the electrodes on the spark plug and the mixture explodes. The spark provided a convenient path for the mixture to move from an unstable but ready state to a stable state (at a much higher entropy) with a large release of energy. This energy release also causes a substantial increase in the entropy of the universe due to the heat transfer from the exploding mixture to the surroundings. The air-gasoline mixture is much like a man standing on the edge of the Grand Canyon. Unless he finds a convenient path, he is not likely

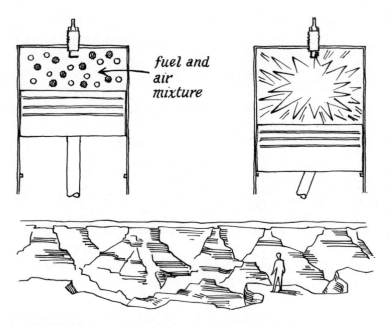

Figure 9-4. The air-gasoline mixture in the cylinder at the left is in an unstable state in which nothing is changing. The spark fires (as is shown on the right), providing a convenient path to allow the energy stored in the fuel-air mixture to be released with a corresponding entropy increase. The man standing at the edge of the Grand Canyon is in an unstable state; however, he is not likely to go voluntarily to the bottom of the Canyon unless a convenient path can be found.

to go voluntarily to the bottom. In this case it is the spark that provides the convenient path. Uranium was in an unstable state for thousands of centuries; then came scientists who built piles, reactors, and bombs to release tremendous energy.

We generalize this concept by noting that all of our power reserves (coal, oil, natural gas, and uranium) are really reserves of negative entropy. These complex and diverse structures stand waiting for man to start the reaction which causes the normal and legitimate increase of entropy to take place.

How does the concept of an unstable state and the second law apply to our earth? We must remember that the earth does not constitute an isolated system. It receives solar energy and is influenced by the gravitational effects of the sun and the moon (hence the tides). Life feeds upon the energy and negative entropy that is being showered on the earth (but it is well to remember that the earth also loses energy to its surroundings). The sun's energy and the rain make crops, the crops provide food, and then living creatures utilize this food to keep on living.

Life acts as the catalytic agent to help destroy unstable states, but at the same time it profits from the destruction by the electricity it receives, the transportation it gets, and so forth. Figure 9–5 illustrates a cycle that follows this scheme. It has long been recognized that some living organisms serve as catalytic agents. Yeasts, for example, are living catalysts which help to overcome certain obstacles and start reactions in a system previously in an unstable state. A catalytic agent cannot violate the second law; all it can do is make something get going that the second law says will happen eventually.

Let us consider for a moment an adult specimen of either a plant or an animal. According to our previous discussion, it is a very complex, highly organized, and improbable system (and hence a system of low entropy) in an unstable state. The instability manifests itself most graphically upon death when suddenly the whole structure, deprived of its "life force," collapses; the organism quickly rots and according to the scriptures goes back to dust from whence it came.

It is this "life force" [6] that appears to act as a *negative catalyst,*

---

[6] *There have been many attempts to show the existence of a life force. No explanation is more interesting (and astounding) than that put forth by Wilhelm Reich, an Austrian psychiatrist who now considers himself a biophysicist. Reich calls the life force* orgone energy, *a nonelectromagnetic force which permeates all of*

The sun's energy is the driving force (negentropy) for photosynthesis that causes crops to grow which . . .

Man harvests . . .

And in some cases he processes the foodstuffs, thereby lowering its entropy.

The man consumes the fruits of his labors which . . .

Allow him to work and . . .

Think and produce . . .

Writings (negentropy) and . . .

Machines (negentropy) and buildings (negentropy), etc.

Figure 9–5. Negentropy at work.

which so long as life goes on maintains the structure in an unstable state, delays the law of increasing entropy, and causes the organism to escape disintegration. This life force slows down the trend toward maximum disorder for a period of time exactly equal to a lifetime. Thus a living creature can be viewed as both a catalyst that releases systems in unstable states (such as the energy reserves mentioned earlier), and at the same time is kept going by some sort of internal anticatalyst. Viewing things in this way, we note that a poison is nothing but an active catalyst while a good drug acts as an anticatalyst.

One of the verifications of the second law that is frequently cited is the observation that the entropy of the foodstuffs consumed by the higher animals is considerably less than the entropy of waste matter of these same animals.[7] The transformation effected by the living system corresponds to an increase in entropy. However, no way has ever been found to measure the entropy of a living organism—simply because a living organism, like a flickering flame, is not a system in equilibrium. Both birth and death are irreversible processes, and there appears to be no way to measure the change in entropy that takes place in an organism at the moments

nature. Blue is the color of orgone energy and he uses it to explain the blueness of the sky, the ocean, deep lakes, and certain frogs when they are sexually excited. In the human body, orgone is the basis of sexual energy; the id of Freud is a bioenergetic concrete form. According to Reich it concentrates in the sexual parts during coitus. At orgasm it flows back again through the entire body. The body charges its red blood cells with orgone energy by breathing. Under the microscope, Reich claims to have detected the "blue glimmer" of red corpuscles as they absorb orgone. We could go on and on about this theory, but we won't.

[7] *Perhaps Josh Billings was correct when he said, "I have finally come to the conclusion that a good, reliable set of bowels is worth more to a man than any quantity of brains."*

of conception or of death. Though we may be able to measure the entropy of an organism just after it dies, this tells us nothing about the organism's entropy just before it died.

So far we have not answered the question posed implicitly at the beginning of this section: What causes one collection of hydrogen, oxygen, carbon, nitrogen, and trace element atoms to form a living cell while another group in exactly the same proportions is nothing more than that—a collection of atoms? Do the scientists in group 1, group 2, or group 3 have the answer? Let us explore this question a little more.

Imagine an engineer who is only familiar with steam engine systems examining an electric motor for the first time. He finds the copper in the form of coils of wire in the armature and rotor pieces; he is familiar with copper but the only use he has seen it put to is in the construction of heat transfer elements in the boilers and condensers of steam-driven systems. He observes iron and steel in the electric motor; the iron forms the core of the armatures and rotors and the steel is used to make the shafts and casings of the motor. The only use he has ever seen for iron and steel is in the steam-driven systems where it is used to form levers, bars, and cylinders. He is convinced that he now sees the same iron, the same steel, and the same copper that he has frequently observed in steam-driven systems. He is also convinced that these materials obey the same laws of nature that he has always utilized, and in that he is right. He can easily see that the steam engine and electric motor operate entirely differently from each other, but he does not suspect that an electric motor is driven by a ghost or by a superphysical agent just because it doesn't use steam or a boiler. Although our fictitious engineer is not familiar with Faraday's principles that govern the operation of an electric motor, he nevertheless recognizes that there may be principles with which he is not familiar.

Following this line of reasoning, many scientists adopt attitudes that place them in group 2. That is, they feel that our present laws of physics and chemistry do not suffice to explain the strange phenomena that are observed when living matter is studied. Something more is needed—they feel that some very important law of nature which has escaped our attention up to now may soon be discovered. Erwin Schrödinger, a Nobel prize-winning physicist, answers the question about whether the new law required to explain the behavior of living matter might not be of a superphysical nature:

> No. I do not think that. For the new principle that is involved is a genuinely physical one: it is, in my opinion, nothing else than the principle of quantum theory over again.

We have asked a lot of questions in this chapter—far more than we have answered. We may have pointed out some of the answers, but there is little that we can say with complete confidence about thermodynamics and life. Stephen Leacock in "Common Sense and the Universe" might have thrown some light on our dilemma when he told the following story. Science, Philosophy and Theology have nowadays all come together—at a funeral. The funeral is that of Dead Certainty. The interment is over and the three turn away together.

> 'Incomprehensible,' murmurs Theology reverently.
> 'What was that word?' asks Science.
> 'Incomprehensible; I often use it in my litanies.'
> 'Ah yes,' murmurs Science, with almost equal reverence, 'Incomprehensible!'
> 'The comprehensibility of comprehension,' begins Philosophy, staring straight in front of him.
> 'Poor fellow,' says Theology, 'he's wandering again; better lead him home.'
> 'I haven't the least idea where he lives,' says Science.
> 'Just below me,' says Theology. 'We're both above you.'

chapter ten
what
else?

A story (perhaps apocryphal) told about Arnold Sommerfeld, a great physicist noted for his clarity of exposition, throws some light on the nature of the study of thermodynamics. During the course of his lifetime, Sommerfeld wrote a series of books, each book covering a particular area: mechanics, optics, electrodynamics, etc. When asked why he had never written a book on thermodynamics, he is reported to have answered in the following way. Thermodynamics is a funny subject. The first time you go through the subject, you don't understand it at all. The second time you go through it, you think you understand it, except for one or two small points. The third time you go through it, you know you don't understand it, but by that time you are so used to the subject, it doesn't bother you any more. When Sommerfeld was killed in an accident, he was in the midst of writing a book on thermodynamics.

That the subject of thermodynamics is not an easy one is a viewpoint that has been held by many eminent scientists. Both Laszlo Tisza and the late Percy Bridgman, physicists of worldwide renown, have expressed themselves on this subject in much the same way. They say that most physicists feel ill at ease with the grand generalizations of thermodynamics and the embarrassingly elementary mathematical concepts applied throughout the discipline. Bridgman summarized it well when he noted:

> It must be admitted, I think, that the laws of thermodynamics have a different feel from most of the other laws of physics. There is something more palpably verbal about them—they smell more of their human origin. The guiding motif is strange to most of physics: namely, a capitalizing of the uni-

versal failure of human beings to construct perpetual motion machines of either the first or the second kind. Why should we expect nature to be interested either positively or negatively in the purposes of human beings, particularly purposes of such unblushingly economic tinge?

Be that as it may, scientists and engineers have consciously and profitably made use of the first two laws of thermodynamics for over a hundred years and the third law for nearly half a century. In this book we have entirely avoided mathematics and largely avoided arithmetic, so that detailed discussion of these applications of thermodynamics is necessarily absent. Possibly more important for many, we have in the space of this book been able to do no more than hint at the tremendous variety of phenomena studied and problems solved by way of thermodynamics. These studies include such diverse areas as the efficient production of substances ranging from life-promoting fertilizers and medicines to life-destroying explosives and poison gases. Thermodynamic investigations are central to our understanding of the effects of pressure and temperature on the velocity of sound in fluids, the elastic properties of rubber, and the operation of storage batteries and fuel cells. All of these and other subjects are discussed extensively in one or more of the books cited in Appendix B, where we have also listed some references to earlier works on the development of thermodynamics.

We shall now briefly examine several aspects of thermodynamics that we have not felt to be central to our exposition, but that do deserve some mention before closing our story.

Thermodynamics is traditionally concerned with the study of phenomena and matter on the macroscopic level. By macroscopic phenomena we mean, for example, reactions and processes that take place in beakers, in cylinders closed by pistons, in distillation columns, etc. Classical thermodynamics does very well in solving important problems connected with these processes, and it does so without any interest in the structure of the matter involved.

The first and second laws of thermodynamics permit derivation of many exact relations between a large number of variables. For instance, classical thermodynamics tells us how the entropy or heat capacity of a gas must depend on the pressure. But classical thermodynamics alone tells us nothing about the actual value of a heat capacity or an entropy. Laboratory measurements must be made to yield the desired numbers. But one of the great attributes of thermodynamics is that just a few data can lead to a tremendous lot of useful derived numbers.

Since thermodynamics is not concerned with the structure of matter, it has the great virtue of being applicable to systems so complicated that we have little understanding of their structures. Thermodynamics is also immune to errors that might result from some misconception about the structure of matter. But since classical thermodynamics is so conveniently independent of the structure of matter, it has to pay the price of being able to contribute little to gaining understanding in this important field. It is much like being unable to have your cake and eat it too.

One of the most satisfying intellectual developments in all of science is statistical thermodynamics, which combines the great generality of classical thermodynamics with detailed molecular theory. The general equations of statistical thermodynamics, largely developed by Maxwell, Boltzmann, and Gibbs, lead to the laws of classical thermodynamics, and in this sense the laws of classical thermodynamics are said to be derivable. It is from these general equations of statistical thermodynamics that we have obtained our ideas about the relations between entropy and molecular order.

But the contribution of statistical thermodynamics extends well beyond providing microscopic understanding of the laws of classical thermodynamics. Since Planck's original development of the quantum theory, Einstein, Debye, Giauque, and others have made use of the resulting understanding to calculate thermodynamic properties of substances from knowledge of the properties of the constituent atoms and molecules. Thus it is now possible to calculate the entropy and heat capacity of a gas from knowledge of masses, geometries, and internal vibrations of the molecules.

We have pointed out earlier that classical thermodynamics is not concerned with the rates of spontaneous processes. That is, classical thermodynamics can define the equilibrium state with great certainty, but it cannot tell us whether that state will be reached from a given set of starting conditions in a second or in a million years. Statistical thermodynamics also offers a way out of this restriction on the range of applicability of classical thermodynamics, but we shall turn here briefly to another approach called irreversible thermodynamics that originated chiefly with Onsager.

Thermodynamics as we have described it in the preceding chapters can only be applied to systems that are in well-defined states—states where the properties are uniform throughout the system. Is there a way to apply thermodynamics to systems that are not in well-defined states because they are changing with time or because they contain gradients of temperature, pressure, or concentration? The answer is a qualified Yes.

The branch of thermodynamics that is applicable to such problems is called *nonequilibrium thermodynamics* or *irreversible thermodynamics*. Its first name is rather obvious since it is applied to the study of systems which are not in equilibrium: that is, they have temperature, pressure, or concentration differences across them. The second name, irreversible thermodynamics, comes about because the unbalanced forces on a system cause irreversible processes to take place. The flow of heat from a high temperature to a low temperature is an irreversible process; heat, according to the second law, will not flow spontaneously from a low temperature to a high temperature. It is important to note that most of the processes of interest in our technologically oriented society are irreversible processes—from the metabolic processes of a living organism to the burning of kerosene in the combustion chamber of a jet engine.

The basic principles of irreversible thermodynamics are the same as those of equilibrium thermodynamics: energy is conserved, and entropy does not decrease. But one must further assume that these laws can be applied locally to every element of the system and that the system is not too far displaced from equilibrium. That is, the irreversible processes must not be taking place too fast.

In utilizing nonequilibrium thermodynamics it has become customary to cast the analysis in terms of flows and forces. The flows generally have a simple physical interpretation—the flow of matter, an electric current, or a heat flow. The forces that drive these flows can be a temperature difference (to drive a heat flow), a pressure difference (to drive a mass flow), a voltage difference (to drive an electric current). Nonequilibrium thermodynamics throws some light on how these forces are related to the flows in certain situations.

At the beginning of the nineteenth century scientists were beginning to note the apparent linear dependence between a force and a flow. J. B. J. Fourier in 1811 observed that the flow of heat was linearly dependent on the temperature gradient (the temperature difference divided by the distance between the hot and cold temperatures). G. S. Ohm found that the magnitude of an electric current is linearly proportional to the voltage difference driving it.

But even before Fourier published his simple linear analysis of heat flow, a Russian colloid chemist had observed a more interesting phenomenon and certainly a more complicated one. F. F. Reuss applied an electric potential across a cell filled with wet clay; to his astonishment he noticed that it produced a flow of water from one of the cell's electrodes. He then reasoned, a priori, that since a liquid flow is normally driven by a pressure difference and he produced one by an electrical potential, that an electrical current should be driven by a pressure difference. He applied a pressure difference to his wet clay cell and detected an electric current. Figure 10–1 illustrates Reuss's experiments.

These electrokinetic experiments were the first to demonstrate the existence of coupled flow phenomena. They established the fact that a flow need not be driven only by its conjugated force but may also be driven by a coupled nonconjugated force. In these experiments Reuss showed that an electric current can be driven by a battery and/or a pressure difference; he also showed that a flow of liquid could be driven by a pressure difference and/or an electrical potential.

It is in the area of coupled phenomena that irreversible thermodynamics has made its most significant contributions. For example, the coupling between a heat flow and an electric current, between the flow of electrolytes and nonelectrolytes through composite membranes, between the flow of heat or electricity in solids whose properties are not uniform in every direction have all been analyzed by means of irreversible thermodynamics.

It is interesting to note that neither classical nor irreversible thermodynamics can predict the magnitude or even the existence of the coupling coefficients which arise in the analyses of coupled phenomena. The laboratory (and in some cases statistical thermodynamics) provides the answers to questions of this nature. In Chapter 1 we mentioned Lars Onsager as one of the leaders in the area of irreversible thermodynamics. His theorem on how the coupling effects for a given system are related indeed forms what is rightly regarded as the cornerstone of nonequilibrium thermodynamics. It goes by the fancy name of the Onsager Reciprocal Relationship and has been verified experimentally many times.

We have tried to outline in a few paragraphs the key ideas of a complicated subject. If we have aroused your interest in this

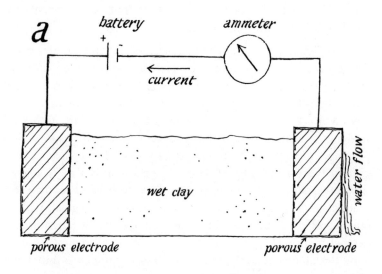

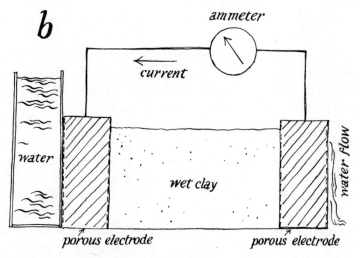

Figure 10–1. Reuss's experiments. In (a) an applied voltage causes a water flow as well as the expected electrical current. In (b) an applied pressure difference causes an electrical current as well as the expected water flow.

subject, you will find some sources that contain additional material on this area in Appendix B.

Thermodynamics has a peculiar sort of fascination for many people, much like dangerous exploration or being a voluntary test subject for a new drug. It is pleasant to read about or to enjoy the benefits that result from someone's actions, but being personally involved is often more frightening than appealing. Nearly all students of science early come to recognize the widespread importance and utility of thermodynamics, but the college underground that involves these same students almost always advises students to study only the minimum thermodynamics required for graduation. Perhaps students find the subject too logical, with so much springing from so little—just as the whole structure of geometry springs from so few axioms. All in all, many students view thermodynamics as something akin to quinine—a bitter pill alleged to have medicinal value.

We have tried to alleviate this taste a bit by conveying a broad sense of meaning and scope to a subject that has for too long been the narrow preserve of scientists. We have tried to do this while distilling the essence of the subject, and yet not becoming bogged down in mathematical or other arguments not absolutely essential to the central issues of thermodynamics.

The path that started with Carnot's idea about how much work can be obtained from heat engines, or Mayer's observation on the color of venous blood in the tropics has taken many turns. Each turn, each twist, was brought about by an idea—an idea that started in a man's head. This is no different from any other branch of science. Henri Poincaré, one of the men who unified the ideas and gave precision to the definitions of thermodynamics at the turn of the century, expressed this very well when he wrote:

> Thought is only a flash between two long nights, but this flash is everything.

We hope you have enjoyed this electrical storm.

appendix A
units of energy and power

The two tables given below are presented to help guide the reader through the maze of units used in thermodynamics. Power is defined as the rate of doing work; thus 1 horsepower represents an energy expenditure of 550 foot-pounds per second.

Units of Energy

unit	abbreviation	definition and/or relation to other units
foot-pound	ft-lb	Energy required to raise 1 lb vertically through 1 ft
calorie	cal	Energy required to raise the temperature of 1 gram of pure water from 14.5 to 15.5°C; equal to 4.184 joules, or 3.088 ft-lb
kilocalorie	kcal	1000 calories
British thermal unit	Btu	Energy required to raise the temperature of 1 lb of water from 60 to 61°F; equal to 778.2 ft-lb or 0.252 kcal
horsepower-hour	hp-hr	2544 Btu or 641.1 kcal
Q		10^{18} Btu or 3.92×10^{14} hp-hr

Units of Power

unit	abbreviation	definition and/or relation to other units
horsepower	hp	550 ft-lb per second
kilowatt	kw	737.6 ft-lb per second or 1.34 hp

appendix B
suggestions for further reading

We have divided these books into three broad categories, with a few words of description for each book.

historical and biographical

Sanborn C. Brown, *Count Rumford* (Garden City, New York: Doubleday and Company, 1962). Biography of Benjamin Thompson, with discussion of his scientific work.

Leo Koenigsberger, *Hermann von Helmholtz* (New York: Dover Publications, 1965). A biography, written by a personal friend, including accounts of both scientific work and cultural activities.

D. K. C. MacDonald, *Faraday, Maxwell, and Kelvin* (Garden City, New York: Doubleday and Company, 1964). Brief biographies of three eminent scientists, with accounts of their work.

Duane Roller, preparer, *The Early Development of the Concepts of Temperature and Heat—The Rise and Decline of the Caloric Theory* (Cambridge, Mass.: Harvard University Press, 1950). Includes parts of original publications, with some illustrative calculations.

Muriel Rukeyser, *Willard Gibbs* (New York: E. P. Dutton, 1964). A comprehensive, nontechnical biography of Gibbs.

cultural

Fred Cottrell, *Energy and Society* (New York: McGraw-Hill Book Company, 1955). Traces the relation between energy, social change, and economic development.

Robert G. Dunlop, Herbert Hoover, Jr., Edward S. Mason, Allan Nevins, and Edward Teller, *Energy and Man* (New York: Appleton-Century-Crofts, 1960). A symposium: Points out the role of energy in the development of industrial nations, with special attention given to fossil fuels.

C. C. Furnas and S. M. Furnas, *Man, Bread and Destiny* (New York: Reynal and Hitchcock, 1937). An interesting introduction to the role that food has played in the development of civilization.

Leslie A. White, *Evolution of Culture* (New York: McGraw-Hill Book Company, 1959). Includes a discussion of the role of energy in the development of culture from anthropoid to present levels.

technical

Stanley W. Angrist, *Direct Energy Conversion* (Boston: Allyn and Bacon, 1965). A review of the methods used to convert heat, light, and mechanical energy to electricity.

Isaac Asimov, *Life and Energy* (New York: Bantam Books, 1965). An introduction to the connections between thermodynamics and living organisms.

Henry A. Bent, *The Second Law* (New York: Oxford University Press, 1965). An introduction to classical and statistical thermodynamics, written with charm and wit.

Harold F. Blum, *Time's Arrow and Evolution* (New York: Harper & Brothers, 1962). A nonmathematical application of thermodynamics to life processes and evolution.

Sadi Carnot, *Reflections on the Motive Power of Fire*, E. Mendoza, ed. (New York: Dover Publications, 1960). An English translation by R. H. Thurston of the original paper by Carnot, along with some of Carnot's notes for future work and important papers on the second law of thermodynamics by Clapeyron and Clausius.

Farrington Daniels, *Direct Use of the Sun's Energy* (New Haven: Yale University Press, 1964). A comprehensive survey of the use of solar energy.

K. G. Denbigh, *The Thermodynamics of the Steady State* (New York: John Wiley and Sons, 1958). An introduction to irreversible thermodynamics.

Loren G. Hepler, *Chemical Principles* (New York: Blaisdell Publishing Company, 1964). An introduction to chemistry, with emphasis on thermodynamics.

Gilbert N. Lewis and Merle Randall, *Thermodynamics* (revised by Kenneth S. Pitzer and Leo Brewer) (New York: McGraw-Hill Book Company, 1961). An up-to-date revision of a classic.

D. K. C. MacDonald, *Near Zero* (Garden City, New York: Doubleday and Company, 1961). An elementary introduction to low-temperature physics.

Morton Mott-Smith, *The Concept of Energy Simply Explained* (New York: Dover Publications, 1964). A nonmathematical introduction to thermodynamics, with interesting historical discussions.

acknowledgments

The authors are grateful to the following for material reproduced in this book.

American Institute of Physics and W. F. Giauque *et al.*: the selection on the word "point" from "Magnetothermodynamic Properties of $MnCl_2$ from $1.3°$ to $4.4°K$ at 90 Kg. A Zero Entropy Reference. The Magnetomechanical Process at Absolute Zero," which appeared in the *Journal of Chemical Physics*, XLII (1965), 1–20, used by permission of the American Institute of Physics and W. F. Giauque.

Harvard University Press: a portion of a drawing on thermometers from *The Early Development of the Concepts of Temperature and Heat* by Duane Roller, used by permission of the Harvard University Press.

Oxford University Press: a selection on the first law from *The Second Law* by Henry A. Bent, used by permission of the Oxford University Press.

Institute of Electrical and Electronics Engineers: a drawing on the use of power in an automobile in the paper "Energy Storage and Conversion," which appeared in the *IEEE Spectrum*, II (1965), 96, used by permission of the Institute of Electrical and Electronics Engineers.

Holt, Rinehart and Winston, Inc.: nine lines from the poem "Mending Wall" from *Complete Poems of Robert Frost*. Copyright 1930, 1939 by Holt, Rinehart and Winston, Inc. Copyright © 1958 by Robert Frost. Copyright © 1967 by Lesley Frost Ballantine. The poems "Under" and "Limited" from *Chicago Poems* by Carl Sandburg. Copyright 1916 by Holt, Rinehart and Winston, Inc. Copyright 1944 by Carl Sandburg. Reprinted by permission of Holt, Rinehart and Winston, Inc. British Commonwealth and Empire, except Canada, rights have been granted by Laurence Pollinger Limited for Jonathan Cape Limited, publishers.

**order
and chaos**

index

index